For Sheila

best wishes &

happy Hallowe'en

Janice MacDonald   Oct '87.

THE NORTHWEST FORT

THE NORTHWEST FORT

FORT EDMONTON

BY JANICE E. MACDONALD

The Publishers:
Lone Pine Publishing
#440, 10113 - 104 St.
Edmonton, Alberta

Typesetting by
Horizon Line Typecraft Ltd.
#440, 10113 - 104 St.
Edmonton, Alberta

Printed and bound in Canada

Design by Terri Guptell

Text and sketches by Janice E. MacDonald

Photos on pages 25, 31, 32, 71, 72, 73, 124 contributed by The Provincial Archives of Alberta
Other photos copyright Lone Pine Publishing

Edited by Grant H. Kennedy

Canadian Cataloguing in Publication Data

MacDonald, Janice E. (Janice Elva), 1959-
  The northwest fort

  Includes index.
  ISBN 0-919433-16-2

1. Fort Edmonton (Alta.) - History. 2. Fort Edmonton (Alta.) - Social life and customs. 3. Fort-
ification - Northwest, Canadian - History. 4. Fort-
ification - Northwest, Canadian - Social life and
customs. 5. Fur trade - Northwest, Canadian.
I. Title.
FC3696.4.M33 1983   971.23'302   C83-091507-9
F1079.5.E3.M33 1983

Dedication

For two strong and special ladies:
my mother and my grandmother
with love and gratitude

Acknowledgements

Many people helped this project on its way by opening doors and giving directions, particularly: Ken Kobylka of Fort Edmonton Park; Shirlee A. Smith of Hudson's Bay Archives; Jan Plosz, Lan Chan-Marples and Jan Switzer, historians at Fort Edmonton Park; Jackie Hobal, supervisor of Social Studies for the Edmonton Public School Board; Jo Toon, Head Librarian of the Historical Resources Library, Province of Alberta Archives; John Gilpin, of Alberta Historic Sites; Jim Parker, Chief Archivist at the University of Alberta; and Anne Martinuk and Kathie Kennedy for editing and proofing.

Still others were indispensible and generous with their time and advice, including: Judy Larmour, James Culkin, Duane Burton and Maurice Marshall.

And then there are those vital people who were always ready with moral support, care and the occasional free meal, especially: Kathy Curley, Jay Culkin, Heather Meyers, Jim Kennison, Frances Leggitt, Judy Larmour, Ken Bolton, Sonya Bobowsky, Bill Williams, Patricia Demers, Michael Hancock, Margaret van de Pitte, Patricia & Roy McIlveen, Lynne van Luven, Dave & Audrey Sands, Grant & Kathie Kennedy, Louise Thompson, Mo Marshall, and my mom – Joyce MacDonald.

I would also like to express my deep gratitude to Helene Hanff – a lady who, through example as well as personal concern, made me open my eyes.

Table of Contents

THE NORTHWEST FORT

ONE
AN HISTORICAL PRELUDE

An Historical Prelude

Fur trading, the industry that explored, exploited, mapped and ruled Canada for two centuries, began as an incidental sideline. After recovering from their disappointment at not finding a passage to the Indies, Europeans discovered great quantities of codfish off the Atlantic coast. Soon fishermen were crossing the Atlantic every summer. The coastal Indians they encountered used fur for clothing, and traded furs with the fishermen for European goods. Trading was of secondary importance, however; and the holds of returning vessels were filled with cod until the early seventeenth century.

Fin gave way to fur as a European demand for fur garments increased. French and Dutch traders traveled inland past the cod banks on the St. Lawrence and Hudson Rivers. Radisson and Grosseilliers, two French Canadians, were among the first to reach the Great Lakes. As they penetrated further, they began to realize that the majority of furs were traded by the Crees from the northern forests. They sailed to France to persuade the King that the easiest access to the treasure trove of the Canadian Shield would be the newly discovered Hudson's Bay.

Louis XIV turned a deaf ear to them, but in England they found Charles II and his cousin Prince Rupert interested in their plan. Rupert outfitted them with two ships, The Eaglet and the Nonsuch, and in 1668 they set out for Hudson's Bay. The Eaglet, with Radisson aboard, had to turn back because of storms, but the Nonsuch arrived in James Bay and Grosseilliers and his crew established Fort Charles. The next spring after trade was conducted, the Nonsuch returned to England loaded with furs.

Charles II granted a royal charter on May 2, 1670, allowing "The Company of Adventurers From England Trading into the Hudson's Bay" all rights to the land whose riverways flowed into the Bay. The area became known as Rupert's Land.

Trade at the Bay cut deeply into the business of the French to the south. Battles were waged over possession of the Bay until The Treaty of Utrecht in 1713 granted sole trading rights in the Bay to the Hudson's Bay Company. Trading went well until independent Canadian traders or *pedlars* began to move further inland. They began to waylay Indians who found it more convenient to trade with the Canadians than to travel the long distance to Hudson's Bay. Under the leadership of such men as Alexander MacKenzie and Simon McTavish, the independent traders joined forces to become the NorthWest Company.

The Hudson's Bay Company, in order to keep its returns from dropping, was forced to follow the North West Company deeper and deeper into the Indian country. For security reasons, the rival trading posts were often housed within the same palisade. By the early 1800's, the companies had reached the Rocky Mountains, and North West Company explorers like Simon Fraser, David Thompson, and Alexander MacKenzie had continued west to the Pacific and north to the Arctic drainage basin.

Rivalry between the two companies became tense. The Hudson's Bay Company was in terrible financial difficulty, and the North West Company wanted access to the Bay. Alexander MacKenzie attempted, with the aid of Lord Selkirk, to buy out the Hudson's Bay Company. His plans backfired, because Selkirk had other plans for the shares he bought in Rupert's Land. He wanted to start a colony of settlers and did not turn over the promised shares to MacKenzie and the Nor'westers.

Liquor became a predominant trade item with both companies. Competition was fierce and tempers ran high. Matters came to a head in 1816, when men from the North West Company ambushed and killed the governor and twenty men from Lord Selkirk's Red River Colony at Seven Oaks.

Both companies gradually recognized that only the Indians were benefiting from their trading wars. The solution was to unify the two companies. An act of British Parliament amalgamated the two companies under the name of the "Hudson's Bay Company" in 1821. Many elements of the North West Company's structure were adopted. Officers, Chief Factors and Traders became partners in the Company. Forty percent of the shares of the company were divided into eighty-five portions. Chief Factors received two shares, Traders one each, and seven shares were set aside as a retirement fund.

The charter of land given the company included Rupert's Land, the area west of the Rocky Mountains (now British Columbia), and the Arctic drainage area.

George Simpson was made governor and he proceeded to reorganize the trading posts to maximum efficiency. Unnecessary posts were closed, the payroll was cut drastically, luxury goods were dropped from the inventory and basic trade routes were decided. The Saskatchewan River became the highway of the fur trade. As well as being the most northwesterly river in the Hudson's Bay drainage system, it was close to the Athabaska River, the major river of the Arctic system. Fort Edmonton was located on the North Saskatchewan, only eighty miles overland from the

Athabaska. It became the vital link between the Columbia and Arctic areas and the Bay.

While it grew steadily for two centuries, the fur trade truly flourished for only a generation. With the advent of silk top-hats, the demands for beaver diminished in Europe, and the land the Company had used exclusively for trapping and trading purposes was now looked to for accommodation for the rising number of immigrants. Canada was given title to the Hudson's Bay Company's holdings in 1870, and Rupert's Land became the Northwest Territories.

TWO
FUR TRADE AND THE NORTHWEST

AND FURTHER WEE DOE BY THESE PRESENTES FOR
OUR HEIRES AND SUCCESSORS MAKE CREATE AND
CONSTITUTE THE SAID GOVERNOR AND COMPANY FOR THE
TYME BEING AND THEIRE SUCCESSORS THE TRUE AND
ABSOLUTE LORDES AND PROPRIETORS OF THE SAME
TERRITORY LYMITTES AND PLACES AFORESAID AND OF
ALL OTHER PREMISSES SAVING ALWAYS THE FAITH
ALLEGIANCE AND SOVERAIGNE DOMINION DUE TO US OUR
HEIRES AND SUCCESORS FOR THE SAME TO HAVE
HOLD POSSESSE AND ENJOY THE SAID TERRITORY
LYMITTES AND PLACES AND ALL AND SINGULER OTHER
THE PREMISSES HEREBY GRANTED AS AFORESAID WITH
THEIRE AND EVERY OF THEIRE RIGHTES MEMBERS
JURISDICCIONS PREROGATIVES ROYALTYES AND
APPURTENANCES WHATSOEVER TO THEM THE SAID
GOVERNOR AND COMPANY AND THEIRE SUCCESSORS FOR
EVER TO BEE HOLDEN OF US OUE HEIRES AND
SUCCESSORS AS OF OUR MANNOR OF EAST GREENWICH IN
OUR COUNTY OF KENT IN FREE AND COMMON SOCCAGE
AND NOT IN CAPITE OR BY KNIGHTES SERVICE
YEILDING AND PAYING YEARELY TO US OUR
HEIRES AND SUCCESSORS FOR THE SAME TWO ELKES AND
TWO BLACK BEAVERS WHENSOEVER AND AS OFTEN AS WE
OUR HEIRES AND SUCCESSORS SHALL HAPPEN TO ENTER
INTO THE SAID COUNTRYES TERRITORYES AND REGIONS
HEREBY GRANTED.

*From the Royal Charter
granted to the
Hudson's Bay Company
by Charles II
May 2, 1670*

Fur Trade and the Northwest

To the uninformed, Canada's choice of a national animal might seem odd. With an abundant choice of majestic animals, why should a country choose to be represented by a tree-gnawing rodent with massive incisors and a paddle-like tail? Ungainly as he may appear, with a European demand for specific furs and felt top-hats, the beaver became to the Canadians what Inca gold had been to the Spaniards.

The fur trade began with a demand for fancy furs such as ermine and marten to be used both as trim and basic material. European needs could easily be filled with the discovery of the Canadian Shield, the greatest fur territory in the world. Its long cold winters ensured that the animals would have thick rich coats throughout most of the year.

While delighting in the glossy pelts, Europeans soon discovered that certain animals possessed a downy undercoat or "wool" that could be put to another use. This wool, separated from the skin and the upper guard hairs became known as "staple fur". It was the raw material for the making of felt hats. Only certain furs were suitable: rabbit, muskrat and, especially, beaver. These animals had underhairs with microscopic barbs that interlocked when the wool was compressed into felt. Beaver hats became so popular that by the eighteenth century staple fur accounted for over sixty percent of all English fur imported. Beaver became the most sought-after fur, and the Hudson's Bay Company came to evaluate all other furs and trade goods in terms of beaver.

In order to understand Canada and her development a study of the fur trade becomes inevitable. For over two hundred years the Northwest was known as Rupert's Land, the domain of the Hudson's Bay Company. The company was entitled by a royal charter to all waterways flowing into the Bay, and they guarded it zealously against other fur companies and would-be settlers. By amalgamating in 1821 with their greatest rivals, the North West Company out of Montreal, they became the most important trading company in North America. Having secured the prize they made every effort to keep it. By spreading rumours that the land they trapped in was totally unfit for farming, they managed to keep settlers from venturing further west than the Red River Settlement (today known as Winnipeg) until the late nineteenth century.

As well as providing employment for every strong and adventurous youth over the age of fourteen, the fur trade was also responsible for a unique method of colonization. The natives they encountered were not shunned or exterminated. They were valued as trappers, traders, guides and interpreters. Many native styles of dress and methods of hunting were copied as being the most suitable to the land. As well, company men began to marry Indian women for their skills and necessary crafts, and to form goodwill between the company and the local tribes. This was unlike the experience of men in other colonized areas where it was taboo to fraternize with native women. The habit eventually died out as

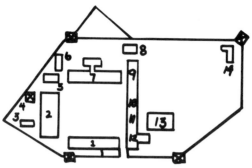

1. Indian House
2. The Big House (Rowand's Folly)
3. Columbia House
4. Watchtower
5. Meat Store
6. Rundle's Chapel & Quarters
7. Bachelor's Hall & adjoining kitchen
8. Ice House
9. Married Men's Quarters
10. Carpenter's/Cooper's Shop
11. Tradesmen's Quarters
12. Blacksmith's Quarters & Shop
13. Boatshed
14. Horse Stable

Fort Edmonton circa 1846

mixed-blood daughters grew to a marriageable age and white "exotics" were brought to the area, but hindsight shows that the native wives of the early explorers and traders were better suited to the rigorous life than their later successors.

Fort Edmonton was situated on Edmonton's present-day legislative grounds. At least the final fort. It was the head office of the entire Saskatchewan District, as well as gateway to the Columbia District across the Rocky Mountains and the Arctic District to the North. York boats, the mainstay vessels of the Hudson's Bay Company were manufactured there; and the bulk of all pemmican, the staple food of the trappers, was made by the women of the fort. Under the leadership of John Rowand, one of the Company's most industrious and colourful Chief Factors, Fort Edmonton became known as the most important fort west of Hudson's Bay.

A close study of Fort Edmonton enables us to infer the lifestyles of the other junior forts of the northwest. Most forts used the French method of a six-sided palisade. This design made for optimal crossfire defence along each wall. A double gate allowed Indians to enter the fort only as far as the Indian House for trading purposes. Bachelor's Hall housed, on the average, twenty clerks; while married couples lived, sometimes three families to a room, along the row of residences connecting with the blacksmith's shop and quarters.

One building not indigenous to all northwest forts was the Big House, known at the time it was built as Rowand's Folly. The grandest house west of Fort Garry, it achieved the required purpose of awing and intimidating the visiting Indians and proclaiming Rowand uncrowned king of his territory along the Saskatchewan.

The royal allusion is not far from the truth. In the heyday of the fur trade, everyone answered to the Chief Factor. The hierarchical structure of a trading post can be compared to the British class system. The Chief Factor occupied the throne, answering only to the governor of the territory. The Chief Traders of the various junior forts took the place of various dukes and lords. The next in line were the Gentlemen, a class of Clerks and minor traders. All other inhabitants of the fort fell into the class of indentured servants. Of course these lines of demarcation were not always so clearly cut. Skilled tradesmen like the blacksmith, carpenter, and cooper held positions slightly above the servant class, but were not considered Gentlemen. At the other end of the scale, various explorers and missionaries existed in an ambiguous social bracket somewhat above the Gentlemen, but always beneath the Factor.

Missionaries were only superficially associated with the Hudson's Bay Company, but played a singular role in fur trade history. Wesleyan Methodists like Robert Terrill Rundle provided the local Indians with a syllabic system of writing their own language, and Jesuit priests like Father Lacombe made a later impact on the area. While respecting these men of God, the company was ambivalent about its responsiblity to the missionaries. Governor Simpson and Chief Factor Rowand did not consider the missionaries to be essential to life within the fort, but had difficulty justifying the support the company gave them when they wandered from the fort to convert the natives. The general theory was that praying Indians would spend less time trapping; and Rowand expressed concern for fort security when Rundle held church services for visiting Indians. It is hard to imagine, when viewing the replica of Rundle's house today, that it could have held, in Rundle's words, "an hundred indians".

Rundle's chapel

The Hudson's Bay Company was functioning at its peak in the early 1840s but, unfortunately, it was just at this time that silk top-hats replaced beaver as the vogue. The bottom fell out of the fur market, and as settlers made inroads into the area, the forts which had at one time dealt in furs turned into conventional trading posts. Fortunately, the locations of the forts along the major waterways gave the Hudson's Bay Company the required edge to maintain their dominion as the major traders of the northwest.

During the era of the fur trade, it is estimated that well over two hundred forts were built. Many of these were abandoned after only one season, and still more were closed after the amalgamation of the North West and Hudson's Bay Companies. While the northwest was divided into several districts, the Saskatchewan District is a useful one to study, as it provides a microcosm of the whole fur enterprise. Fort Edmonton, at the western end of the mighty North Saskatchewan River, was discovered to be the perfect gateway to both the northern Arctic areas, and the Pacific districts across the Rocky Mountains. As such, it became the administrative centre for much of the northwest.

Several junior forts fell under the jurisdiction of Fort Edmonton. Fort Assiniboine, eighty miles northwest of Edmonton, began its existence as an outpost fort in the Lesser Slave Lake District, but in 1824 became part of the Saskatchewan District. When George Simpson ordered the Assiniboine Trail made, Fort Assiniboine took on the character of a waystation where the brigades changed from horses to boats.

Instead of a Chief Factor or Trader, Fort Assiniboine was managed usually by a Clerk or postmaster, which indicates its status as an important post. Often the manager would be housed at Fort Edmonton, commuting to his post only when needed. According to the reports of various travellers there must have been four or five whitewashed buildings surrounded by a low palisade, in accordance with the fact that the neighbouring Indians were relatively non-threatening.

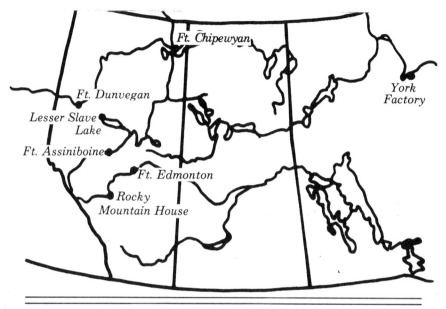

Significant forts in the northwest

Brigades for the Columbia and New Caledonia Districts across the Rocky Mountains would travel together as far as Fort Assiniboine, where they would split forces — the Columbians crossing the Rockies by way of the Athabaska Pass to Boat Encampment, where they joined the Columbia River to Fort Vancouver, and the New Caledonians following the Miette River to Leather or Yellowhead Pass and at Tete Jaune Cache taking either the Fraser to Fort George, or the Nechako River to Fort St. James.

As soon as the Columbia and New Caledonia brigades were serviced the pack-horses bringing supplies for Lesser Slave Lake would arrive at Fort Assiniboine. From there they were taken by boat down the Athabaska River, and then up Lesser Slave Lake to the post.

Lesser Slave Lake post, one hundred and thirty miles northwest of Fort Edmonton had, at one time, been headquarters for Jasper House and another temporary post. Once travel ceased to come from the Bay via Ile-a-la-Crosse, Lesser Slave Lake became part of the Saskatchewan District. The Chief Trader there, William Connolly, was made Chief Factor of the New Caledonia District. While it continued to bring in a fair quota of furs, it was not considered a major post.

The most southwesterly fort of the Saskatchewan District was Rocky Mountain House. Its history is one of many openings and closures. Often it operated only seasonally, with no one wintering in the fort. Chief Factor Rowand considered it necessary to accommodate the Piegan Indian trade, but, situated so near to fractious and war-like Indians, it was built with double palisades and extreme caution was used in trading.

Paul Kane described it thus:

> It is built like most of the other forts, of wood, but with more than ordinary regard to strength, which is thought necessary on account of the vicious disposition of the Blackfoot tribe...
> — Paul Kane, *Wanderings of an Artist.*
> London: 1859; Toronto: 1925) p. 287

Rocky Mountain House was eventually closed permanently in 1875.

Fort Edmonton shared many similarities with Fort Chipewyan, but the administrative centre of the northern Athabaska District had its own distinctive features. Fort Chipewyan had no need for high palisades; the Indians who traded there were peaceful. Fort Edmonton enjoyed easier access routes, however, and continued to flourish long after its sister fort to the north.

Each fort evolved its own special character according to four major factors: its location, the environment, the abundance of fur

Fort Chipewyan

in the area, and the type of Indians who traded there. A small post like Fort Dunvegan could not boast a boat yard, a pemmican supply house, or an administrative function. Located as it was, however, in the fertile Peace River Valley, it was renowned as a market garden, supplying neighbouring posts with fresh vegetables.

Fort Dunvegan

Fort Edmonton Park,
1975

Fort Edmonton with its prime location, varied trade-related activities, relative importance in the Company network and colourful characters, lends itself admirably to study as the prototypical northwest fort. It was situated on the borderline between the peaceful Woods Indians and the war-like Plains tribes, maintaining an uneasy peace (for the most part) between the Cree and their enemies, the tribes of the Blackfoot Confederacy.

This fort became, in time, the major administrative centre of the northwest. As well, many of the people who lived or visited within its palisades are now legendary.

Bastion and post-on-sill palisade, Fort Edmonton Park

Today an accurate replica of Fort Edmonton stands two miles upriver of the original (final) site. Built with agonizing attention detail, Fort Edmonton Park provides the visitor with an immediate picture of the atmosphere of a northwest fort.

THREE
John Rowand, Chief Factor

No. 19

ABOUT 46 YEARS OF AGE. ONE OF THE MOST PUSHING BUSTLING MEN IN THE SERVICE WHOSE ZEAL AND AMBITION IN THE DISCHARGE OF HIS DUTY IS UNEQUALLED, RENDERING HIM TOTALLY REGARDLESS OF EVERY PERSONAL COMFORT AND INDULGENCE. — WARM HEARTED AND FRIENDLY TO AN EXTRAORDINARY DEGREE WHERE HE TAKES A LIKING, BUT ON THE CONTRARY HIS PREJUDICES EXCEEDINGLY STRONG. OF A FIERY DISPOSITION AND BOLD AS A LION. — AN EXCELLENT TRADER WHO HAS THE PARTICULAR TALENT OF ATTRACTING THE FIERCEST INDIANS TO HIM WHILE HE RULES THEM WITH A ROD OF IRON AND SO DARING THAT HE BEARDS THEIR CHIEFS IN THE OPEN CAMP WHILE SURROUNDED BY THEIR WARRIORS: HAS LIKEWISE A WONDERFUL INFLUENCE OVER HIS PEOPLE. — HAS BY SUPERIOR MANAGEMENT REALIZED MORE MONEY FOR THE CONCERN THAN ANY THREE OF HIS COLLEAGUES SINCE THE COALITION; AND ALTHO' HIS EDUCATION HAS BEEN DEFECTIVE IS A VERY CLEAR HEADED FELLOW. — WILL NOT TELL A LIE PUBLICK IS VERY UNCOMMON IN THIS COUNTRY BUT HAS SUFFICIENT ADDRESS TO EVADE THE TRUTH WHEN IT SUITS HIS PURPOSE; FULL OF DROLLERY AND HUMOUR AND GENERALLY LIKED AND RESPECTED BY INDIAN SERVANTS AND HIS OWN EQUALS.

George Simpson referring
to John Rowand in his
private Character Book

John Rowand, Chief Factor

Although he stood no higher than five foot six, Chief Factor John Rowand was known as "the Big Mountain" to the Indians he traded with. What he lacked in height Rowand made up in charm, bluster and sheer force of personality. Fort Edmonton, once known as the most unruly post in all of Rupert's Land became the most important fort west of York Factory under his leadership. Important men like Sir George Simpson counted him a personal friend. His men feared his temper and loathed his demands for complete servitude, but no one could remain indifferent to him. He built himself the grandest house in the west, lavishly lighted through *glass* window panes shipped from England in barrels of molasses. He also spared no expense on his greatest passion – horse racing. The powerful Chief Factor built a race course near the fort and began breeding the finest stock of horses in the territory. Operating during the zenith of the fur trade, John Rowand epitomized the true Gentleman of the Company of Adventurers.

Rowand was born in 1789, the son of a Belfast-born Montreal

John Rowand

physician. He signed on with the North West Company at the age of fourteen. A promising boy, he was sent as an apprentice clerk to Fort Augustus, the N.W.C. post that shared a palisade with its H.B.C. rival, Edmonton House. Rowand spent two years at Ft.

Augustus, was sent for a year to Ft. Vermillion, spent some time in Bas de la Riviére and, in 1806, found himself back in Fort Augustus. By the time he was made Chief Factor in 1826, he had a thorough knowledge of the entire Saskatchewan District.

With the amalgamation of the Hudson's Bay Company and the North West Company in 1821, many Nor'westers were placed in significant positions of authority in the new Company. Governor Simpson apparently concluded that the hardy Nor'westers had a better understanding of the area than the Hudson's Bay Gentlemen. He promoted John Rowand to Chief Trader under the leadership of James Sutherland, Chief Factor of the Saskatchewan District. Rowand was placed in charge of Rocky Mountain House for the winter season of 1821-22. He took charge of Edmonton House for the summer of 1822. With the appointment of Colin Robertson as new Chief Factor of the District, Rowand and Donald MacKenzie were sent south to the Bow River District to determine if southern expansion might be in order. They reported few beaver, and the move south was judged futile. In consequence Fort Edmonton remained the centre of the prairie trade.

Governor Simpson, an intrepid traveller, first met Rowand during this southern reconnaisance. Simpson had come out to Chesterfield House, the base fort of the Bow River Expedition, to see for himself whether a move was advisable. He and Rowand became immediate friends, recognizing in each other a kindred determination and will to leadership. Rowand was promoted to Chief Trader and resumed his residence in Fort Edmonton.

In 1824, Governor Simpson decided on a new transcontinental route up the Saskatchewan River to Ft. Edmonton, and overland to Fort Assiniboine and the Athabaska River. This decision was due to the fact that Rowand had beaten Simpson to the Ft. Assiniboine area by heading home down the Saskatchewan from the annual council meetings and trekking overland to meet him. Although Simpson did not acknowledge Rowand in his decision, he did speak highly of him in a dispatch dated August 1, 1825:

...Mr. Rowand's, very superior management at Edmonton which is, without exception, the most troublesome post in the Indian country does him much credit. He and the situation seem made for each other and the high order in which I found everything connected with his charge as I passed this way this spring excited both my surprise and my admiration.

It is not surprising, therefore, that John Rowand found himself promoted to Chief Factor of the Saskatchewan District the next summer.

By the time Rowand was made Chief Factor, Edmonton House had already been relocated three times. A flood in 1829 forced yet another move from the river flats (where the Rossdale Power plant may now be found) to its final location on the bluff where the legislative grounds are today. By 1846, the Big House was complete and Fort Edmonton, the "kingdom" fit for the "czar of the prairies" was much the way it is shown by the replica in Fort Edmonton Park.

Rowand took a Metis wife, named Louise Umphrieville, and although their vows were never consecrated, he never left her. He chose instead to make her chatelaine of the grandest house west of Fort Garry, and the seven children they reared together were given every opportunity in a world where mixed-blood children were often forgotten or relegated to minor positions in the Company structure.

Through droughts and prairie fires, lean times and years of planty, Rowand contined to reinforce Fort Edmonton's reputation as the most productive fort in the territory. Under his supervision it became more than just a trading post; it was a central depot for fur storage, the location of all York boat manufacture, a breeding farm for pack-horses and the gateway to the Columbia District beyond the Rocky Mountains.

Simpson's trust in Rowand was not misplaced, and it grew to such an extent that when Simpson decided to make his global tour, Rowand was invited to join him for part of the distance. This gesture was only partly to reward Rowand for excellence within the Service. Simpson was well aware of the Indians' respect for Rowand, and knew that Rowand's presence would guarantee the party safe passage to the Pacific.

Rowand accompanied Simpson to Alaska, down the coast to Santa Barbara and, finally, on the sixteen-day trip to the Sandwich Islands (today known as the State of Hawaii). Being the first Edmontonian to escape the long cold winter in Hawaii might classify Rowand as a trendsetter, but he was seemingly happy to return to his own environment where he resumed dominion until his death in 1854.

Frances, Sir George Simpson's young bride, said of Rowand upon meeting him that, "He is a remarkably lively good tempered man, with a countenance which bespeaks drollery and good humour." While he may have presented this face to the ladies, or at any rate the Governor's Lady, as Rowand grew older he extracted servitude from his men at the expense of their affection. An old leg injury turned into a pronounced limp, and the rhythm he created as he stamped about was the inspiration for his nickname of "Twenty-one Shillings", or "One-Pound-One". His winning and ready charm was fading, being replaced more and more with sheer bluster. He was not blind to the change, however, and in a letter to fellow Factor Donald Ross dated 1851 he wrote:

> I make difficulties where there are none; people
> after being so long in the service get useless.

Louise, his partner for thirty-nine years, died in 1849, and Rowand began to consider retirement. Simpson, knowing it would be difficult to replace a man of Rowand's calibre, urged him to think carefully about retirement, and to consider relocation to the Red

River Settlement over retirement to Montreal or England. In Simpson's opinion, a man like Rowand would never accustom himself to the overly refined air of civilization after fifty years in the comparative wilderness.

Rowand's career was coming to a close, and a parallel comparison could be made to the fur trade in general. Company men were being lured to California with the reports of gold discovered at Sutter's Mill. Rowand exposed a reflective side of his character in a letter to Donald Ross on the subject of the Gold Rush:

> Out of the Company servants who deserted last spring no less than five found a grave on arriving at the Gold mines – many die and many do not, but where is the country where people do not die –

In the spring of 1854, Rowand again led the brigade downriver to York Factory. His plan was to take a year's furlough in Montreal as a step toward easing into retirement. The brigade stopped at Fort Pitt, where his son, John Jr., was Chief Trader. On the morning of the departure, Rowand came upon two of his voyageurs fighting. His own temper rising, stepped between them to quell the argument. His legendary temper got the better of him, and he dropped dead of what reports would indicate to be a massive heart attack. He was buried quietly at Fort Pitt, accompanied by the mourning of his son and fellow Gentlemen, and the joy and relief of his indentured servants. When news of his death reached Sir George Simpson, the Governor of the Hudson's Bay Company wrote:

> With him, it may be said, the old race of officers is extinct, . . . I trust I may be permited to record my personal tribute of regard for the memory of an old and staunch friend, from whom both in public and a private capacity I

ever received a firm and consistent support - ...
He was a man of sterling integrity and a warm
heart and was not surpassed by any Officer in
the service for unswerving devotion to the
public interest.

If Rowand's life was filled with the things legends are made of,
it was nothing compared to the events that followed his death. Sir
George Simpson, knowing of his friend's desire to be buried in
Montreal, made plans to have his bones disinterred. His body was
rendered down by an Indian who had to be kept drunk all day to
stir the cauldron, and while the women made soap with the rest,
the bones of John Rowand were packed in rum as a preservative
and placed in a barrel marked "salt pork".

Simpson placed the cask in his canoe, and took it with him as
far as the Red River Settlement. Then, fearing that superstitious
voyageurs might discover the contents of the barrel and heave it
overboard, he had it sent to York Factory where it was placed on a
ship for England. Once across the ocean, it was loaded onto
another ship for Montreal and finally – four years after his death –
John Rowand was placed in Mount Royal Cemetery in a plot of
honour next to Frances, Sir George's late wife.

Story has it, however, that when the cask was finally opened
the liquid surrounding the bones turned out to be water, not the
original rum. Visions of company servants discovering the true
contents of their cargo and drinking the old man's health with the
same rum that surrounded his remains are the fodder of spicy
legends, the sort Rowand himself would probably have greatly enjoyed. And if legends make for immortality, it is no less than this
man deserved, for he was larger than life in an era when adventure
became the norm.

FOUR
ROWAND'S FAMILY

I WAS RECEIVED BY MR. ROWAND, WIDELY KNOWN AMONG THE PLAIN INDIANS AS THE "BIG MOUNTAIN"; HE WAS A POWERFUL BUT NOT VERY TALL MAN OF ROUGH DETERMINED ASPECT, AND VERY NEAR LAME FROM AN EARLY ACCIDENT. HUNTING ALONE AS A YOUNG MAN HE HAD BEEN THROWN FROM HIS HORSE AND HAD BROKEN HIS LEG. BY SOME MEANS INTELLIGENCE REACHED THE FORT OF WHAT HAD OCCURED AND BEFORE THE WHITES COULD DO ANYTHING AN INDIAN GIRL HAD MOUNTED AND GALLOPED OFF IN THE DIRECTION INDICATED. SHE FOUND HIM, AND SAVED HIS LIFE AND HE MARRIED HER.

1844, Sir Henry Lefroy
from "Journey to the
North-West". Trans. Roy.
So., Can. Sect. 11:67-96,
1938

Rowand's Family

In 1810 Rowand met the woman he was to spend the next twenty-nine years of his life with. A mixed-blood woman living with the Indians camped outside the fort, her name was Louise Umphrieville. The story of their meeting is probably the most romantic in fur trade annals. Apparently Rowand went off hunting alone one day, with no one in the fort paying much attention to the direction in which he was heading. When his horse returned alone, the only person who could accurately search for him was the young Indian girl who had been keeping her eye on the pleasant-looking bachelor. She found him with a broken leg, nursed him back to health, and he took her as his wife. Together they had seven children: John Jr., Sophia, Alexandra, Nancy, Henry, Marguerite, and Adelaide.

Life in the northwest was hard. It was laboriously hard for women who were allotted all the menial tasks. In these circumstances, the role of Factor's wife implied a comparative life of luxury. Louise Rowand was chatelaine of the largest house west of Fort Garry. Her husband was an influential man in the Company and a great personal friend of Governor Sir George Simpson. Simpson's friendship with Rowand might account for an apparent restraint in mentioning Louise in his writings. Although he himself had two or three country wives, Simpson did not take kindly to the wives of his men. Mentions of one man's "bit of brown" and another's "copper beauty" dot his journals. That Louise escaped labels of this kind might be an indication of Simpson's respect.

Louise was responsible for the care of the Big House, Rowand himself, and their large family. She had servants under her charge as well. As wife of the factor she would in some measure also be responsible for overseeing the working women of the fort. Even with these tokens of responsibility, she was required to eat with the children and other women in a separate dining room off the kitchen; never with the men in the great hall.

Fine embroidery and beadwork would keep her hands busy, but without a doubt her mind must have dwelt on the possibility that she could be usurped at any time. Rowand mentions in his correspondence that he was thinking of retiring and taking a white wife, like his friends Simpson, McTavish and Hargraves. Louise must have wondered each time he left with the brigade for York Factory whether he would return that fall with an English "exotic" in tow.

In spite of Rowand's daydreams, a white wife never materialized. When Louise died in 1849, John Rowand wrote, "my old friend, the Mother of all my children is no more." She was buried in the river flats, under what is now 105 St. in Edmonton and John Rowand never took another wife.

Children of the mixed-blood "country" marriages of the northwest were often at a disadvantage when their fathers left the territory, but John Rowand's family seems to have fared remarkably well.

John Rowand Jr.

John Jr., the eldest son, signed on as a youth with the Hudson's Bay Company, and eventually became Chief Trader of Fort Pitt under his father's jurisdiction. From all reports he had inherited the Rowand bluster but not the charm. He was never as well liked as his father. In 1848 he married Margaret Harriott, his brother-in-law James' daughter from an earlier tragic marriage.

Rowand's father had been a physician. Accordingly he sent his second son, Alexander, east for medical training. The young man became a favourite with Sir George and Lady Frances Simpson, and accompanied the Governor on his round-the-world excursion.

Alexander studied medicine in Edinburgh. While he was there, rumours began to circulate that he had developed a taste for high living. Rowand and Simpson were both disappointed in his lifestyle, and eventually began to refuse his requests for money as he travelled fpom Paris to London in reputed indolence. Alexander eventually returned to Canada and set up practice in Quebec City.

Henry, the youngest son, was sent to the Red River School at the age of fourteen, and tragically died two years later of "suffusion of the brain, a strange and deadly malady".

John Rowand provided for his sons in a manner much superior to that of many of the Company Gentlemen, Sir George Simpson included. His attitude toward the education and futures of his daughters, while predictably of secondary importance to that concerning his sons, was also remarkably cultivated. His second eldest daughter, Nancy, was legally married to his trusted friend and Chief Trader, James Harriott, and installed as the first lady of Rocky Mountain House.

Harriott's first wife had been driven mad by the knowledge that she had rolled over and crushed her newborn child in her sleep. Crazed with grief, she had seized a horse and ridden off into the wilderness. She was never seen again. Harriott was left to care for his small daughter, Margaret. Nancy gave him six more children in their seventeen years of marriage, but predeceased him at the age of thirty-two.

The Rowand girls who remained at home, Sophia, Marguerite and Adelaide, were given a rudimentary education by visiting missionaries, most notably by the Reverend Robert Rundle. Although they lived in the Big House and were the daughters of an English "Gentleman of the Company", they had little contact with their father and his guests. Father Lacombe wrote of them that "they were truly half breeds and understood nothing but the Cree language, but each one of them had been instructed well in their religious instructions."

After their mother's death in 1849 the girls were sent to the convent of the Grey Nuns in St. Boniface. It was Rowand's wish that, after his death, they be sent to live with Alexander. None ever ventured further east than the Red River Settlement. Adelaide apparently planned to become a nun, but died before she took the vows. Sophia and Marguerite returned to the northwest to live with John Jr. and his wife. Marguerite eventually married James MacKay, who was to become the first lieutenant-governor of the province of Manitoba. Sophia remained single.

Sophie's room

View from Sophie's room

Gazing into the re-creation of Sophia's small room in the front corner of the Big House in Fort Edmonton Park, it is easy to imagine the thoughts occupying the mind of John Rowand's unmarried eldest daughter. As it was, she lived in relative luxury, but her fortunes might rapidly change were her father to retire from the territory. She had no tribe to return to, like the women a generation before her; and no Company husband to keep her sheltered at the fort. Since she had not found a husband among the plethora of men at the fort during her youth, she was not likely to retain any hopes of marriage as she grew older.

Sophia was lucky to have been born to John Rowand. Though in his will he referred to his children as *reputed* (meaning born out of wedlock), he left £7,500 each to Sophia, Marguerite and Adelaide, and £3,000 each to John Jr. and Alexander. According to the terms of the will, John Jr. was also to receive the residue of his estate, both real and personal; and should any of the heirs die without issue, their share was to be divided among the survivors.

FIVE
CLERKS

"CLASS...BETWEEN INTERPRETERS AND CLERKS."

...WE HAVE REMOVED TO THIS CLASS SEVERAL PERSONS FROM THE LIST OF CLERKS WHO WERE NOT QUALIFIED TO PERFORM THE DUTIES OF THE SITUATIONS THEY NOMINALLY FILLED AND OTHER VACANCIES HAVE BEEN FILLED UP BY YOUNG MEN THE HALFBREED SONS OR RELATIONS OF GENTLEMEN IN THE COUNTRY WHO COULD NOT OBTAIN ADMISSION TO THE SERVICE AS APPRENTICE CLERKS. THOSE WHO ENTER THE SERVICE IN THIS CLASS...HAVE NO PROSPECT OF FURTHER ADVANCEMENT, NOR IS IT INTENDED THAT THEY SHALL BE REMOVED FROM THIS CLASS EXCEPT IN VERY PARTICULAR CASES OF GOOD CONDUCT COUPLED WITH VALUABLE SERVICES.

George Simpson, 1832
(Williams 1975: 232)

CLERKS

If a young man came from a good family and yearned for the adventure of the northwest, it was likely he would join the Company as an apprentice clerk, with dreams of working his way up the company ladder in the same fashion as John Rowand and others before him. Unfortunately, with the new strictures imposed by Governor Simpson, a young man would need to display exceptional service in order to forward himself in the ranks. Under Simpson's leadership, the Service was cut drastically in manpower, as well as luxuries for officers being reduced. Service in the Company might no longer have been a career-building venture, but since a young man walked out of the wilds with nearly all his pay in savings (there being nothing to spend it on in the northwest) time spent in the employ of the Hudson's Bay Company was still considered time well spent.

Unmarried clerks were housed in Bachelor's Hall, along with twenty to thirty other men. The Hall had its own kitchen and din-

The Great Hall at Fort Edmonton

58. *The Northwest Fort*

ing area, and the men had their meals prepared by a cook who lived in the room adjoining the kitchen. The main dining area of the Hall was also the location of the occasional dances which took place at the fort.

Trading took place at two main times during the year, and trading procedures varied with each trading party. Woods Indians like the Cree or Assiniboine around the area, and the half-breed freemen who depended on the fort for their provisions usually did their trading on credit shortly after the supplies had arrived from York Factory. Their accounts were settled in late winter, when they brought in the product of their hunts. More mobile tribes like the Plains Cree were treated with deference, and courted by the clerks who knew that these Indians could just as easily ride south and trade with the Americans. Trading then became a ceremonial procedure, with the raising of the fort flag and a salvo from the bastion guns announcing the arrival of the chiefs. Peace pipes would be smoked, speeches made and ceremonial gifts exchanged before the actual trading would begin.

Tribes which had the reputation of being volatile were treated with more caution. These tribes, namely those of the Blackfoot Confederacy – Blackfoot, Sarcee, Bloods, Piegans – were also highly mobile and had to be cossetted for trading purposes; yet since they were more unruly, security precautions had to be taken. Furs, pemmican, grease, buffalo robes, meat and other returns were evaluated by company clerks and taken immediately to the fur loft. The Indians were given tokens of wood known as *made beaver* or sticks known as *castors* of the same value, and were then allowed to trade their tokens at the wicket rather than enter the trade room proper.

Made beaver stood for the estimated value of a prime beaver pelt on the London market, and it became the standard accounting unit for the Hudson's Bay Company. All trade goods and all pelts and returns from the Indians were assigned made beaver standards. For instance, by the Company's standard, it would take six muskrat pelts to equal one made beaver token, while one wolverine pelt would net two made beavers. Conversely, an Indian could buy twelve needles with one made beaver token, but would have to pay seven tokens for a Hudson's Bay blanket.

In order to maintain consistency in trading while relative values of furs in London changed from season to season, the Company Standard remained quite constant over time. However, it was common practice at each post to employ a slightly higher standard than the one predetermined by the Company, and this was known as the Factor's Standard. Measurements would be made with the Clerk's thumb weighing down the scale, and brandy and rum might be diluted with water. Some traders might insist on twelve muskrat skins to make one made beaver token, and demand eight tokens for a blanket. The extra amount earned while trading was recorded as the *Overplus*, a slush fund against which peace offerings and ceremonial gifts were charged.

The Fur Loft was located above the Trade Room, and all furs were placed there immediately after trading. Small furs were hung up, larger ones laid in piles on the floor, and all were checked periodically through the winter to see they dried properly. The Clerk's responsibility, when trading was not taking place, was to detail, weigh and assemble the furs into *pieces* weighing approximately ninety pounds each. A *piece* was a bale of furs which had been packed within a frame and bound with cord. A stave of wood detailing every article within the bale was packed with it. When the time drew near for the brigade to depart for York Factory, each bale was taken to the fur press located just outside the Trading Store and compacted by the combined pressure of two or three men into a uniform size some two feet high and a foot-and-a-half square. The pieces were then covered with burlap and lashed with cord, another stave of wood tied to the outside detailing their origin. A voyageur on portage would be expected to carry two pieces, one in front and one slung across his back, as well as to maneuver a canoe above his head.

Fur press

Clerks in Fort Edmonton, since it was the central supply depot for all the minor posts as well, were responsible for the safe arrival and good condition of all furs passing through their jurisdiction. Most bales arriving from junior posts were merely stored until the spring run, but any bales which were found to be wet or improperly packed were recounted and repacked in the Fort Edmonton fur loft.

The following lists demonstrate the volume of furs handled by the clerks of Fort Edmonton. The first list represents half a season's trading at Fort Edmonton, and was taken from the Edmonton Post Journals dated December 31, 1832.

> 24 badgers
> 116 bear
> 681 beaver
> 13 fisher
> 45 fox

17 lynx
58 marten
40 mink
2592 musquash (muskrat)
87 otter
17 wolverine
880 wolves
756 swan skins
81 buffalo
900 moose
121 buffalo robes

This amount of furs would translate by weight into approximately one hundred and seventy-nine pieces. But while Fort Pitt and Fort Carleton took on some of the responsibility of processing for the district, the clerks at Fort Edmonton were responsible for the bulk of all furs departing from the Saskatchewan district, and in 1846 the totals were listed as the following:

237 badger
396 black bear
91 brown bear
72 grey bear
1202 large beaver
664 small beaver
547 fisher
52 silver fox
164 cross fox
684 red fox
3049 kit fox
3255 lynx
4488 martens
12393 musquash
98 otter
7017 wolves

20 wolverine
342 buffalo robes
75 calf buffalo robes
462 whole buffalo dressed skins
280 half buffalo dressed skins
432 whole buffalo parchment skins
44 half buffalo parchment skins
1186 elk and red deer dressed skins
3 jumping deer dressed skins
9400 goose quills
950 swan quills
231 swan skins

To those entering it for the first time, the Trade Store must have seemed a veritable treasure house. Warm rich scents of spices and tobacco mingled with the pervasive smell of drying furs in the loft upstairs; bright, cheerful colours of Hudson's Bay point blankets reflecting in the surfaces of shiny brass kettles and copper pots; the chime-like sound of glass beads brushing against each other; a visit to the Trade Room could invoke a pleasurable response from senses sharpened to a fine edge by the harsh environment. Beads, blankets, guns, tobacco — with the right number of made beaver tokens a man could live like a king.

Beads, one of the goods most in demand, were manufactured of glass in Italy and Bohemia. Once they had arrived in the new land, they were removed from the boxes thay had been shipped in and sold either by the string or by the pound. Seed beads, the smallest variety, were the ones used to the greatest extent in the intricate beadwork of garments. Although they ordinarily required jeweller's needles to work them, the Indians' thread made of sinew could be stretched fine enough to accommodate the beads, and the end of the sinew was used as the needle to pick up the beads. While a regular needle was used to make holes in the cloth or leather being adorned, the handy sinew "thread and needle in one" was used to stitch and weave them into patterns.

Larger beads were used for necklaces and jewellery and finery pieces for the Indians' horses. Known occasionally as *pony beads*, they were sold by the pound and came in colours of red, black, white and blue. Blue was the predominant colour of all beads because it seemed to be the bestselling favourite of the western Indians.

Point blankets became a trademark of the Hudson's Bay Company at a very early date. Although the multi-striped blankets are the most easily recognizable, they were also (and still are) made in colours of caramel, white, green and red. When each individual blanket was woven by a separate waever, there was difficulty is standardizing the symbols of weight and size. After 1850 a standard indigo-blue band was woven across each end of a blanket, denoting by its width (anywhere from two to five-and-a-half inches) the weight of the particular blanket.

These blankets were also the material eventually used to make the *capotes* or hooded cloaks that were sold at the posts. Legend has it that the blankets were first used to make capotes during the War of 1812, when greatcoats for the soldiers were at a premium. The white blankets made for good camouflage in the winter. A capote might be compared in style to today's parka, imagining it to come to slightly above the knees and to be tied with an Assomption sash. Imagine moccasined feet, and leggings sewn from another blanket. Then sling a gun over the man's shoulder and set him on snowshoes, and you would have a visible picture of a backwoods trapper in mind.

The Assomption sash, or *ceinture flechée*, was named after its weavers in L'Assomption, Quebec. Every member of every class of the fur trade owned one and wore it wrapped about his waist, tied with the fringed ends swinging at his side. A sash was a necessary part of any man's finery, but the longer it was and the more times he could wrap it around his waist spoke of both his style and his affluence when he wore it.

The Hudson's Bay Trade Stores stocked clay pipes and several types of tobacco: Carat, Cavendish, Negro Head, Irish Roll, Canada Twist and Havana Cigars. Cuban cigars in the wilds of the Canadian Shield might seem like luxury, but there were other items at the posts which were considered not only necessary but essential.

Guns were an important trading item at the forts. The Hudson's Bay Company dealt in two qualities of gun, one for the employees of the Company and one for trade. Although the Company rifles were thought to be superior, neither was infallible. The

Brass dragon found on H.B.C. trade guns

guns were of a flintlock system with a smooth bore, and that did not make for deadly accuracy of the musket balls they fired.

Knives were also much in demand, and the Company made great profits by trading on their practical uses. Copper and cast iron pots and kettles were prized for making cooking easier. Axes and needles, as well as other less practical items like buttons, crosses and small metal animals also sold well.

All in all, though the incoming of the white man may have changed the Indian's lifestyle forever, for a certain time during the heyday of the fur trade the items the natives received from contact with the white men moved their civilization toward its apex. Horses, guns and knives all contributed toward making the Indians more powerful and prosperous within their own traditions and mores.

SIX
SKILLED TRADESMEN

OH, A BLACKSMITH COURTED ME
I'D N'A MAN SEEN BETTER
HE FAIRLY WON MY HEART,
WROTE ME A LETTER
WITH HIS HAMMER IN HIS HAND
HE LOOKED SO CLEVER
AND IF I WERE WITH MY LOVE
I'D LIVE FOREVER.

OH, WHERE HAS MY LOVE GONE
WITH HIS CHEEKS LIKE ROSES?
HE'S GONE ACROSS THE SEA
GATHERING PRIMROSES
I'M AFRAID THE SHINING SUN
MIGHT BURN AND SCORCH HIS BEAUTY
AND IF I WERE WITH MY LOVE
I'D DO MY DUTY.

"The Blacksmith"
Trad. Anon
British Isles

SKILLED TRADESMEN

In the Company's hierarchy tradesmen fell below the level of Clerks. The cooper, blacksmith, carpenters and York boat builders were, however, among the most valuable men found at any northwest fort. The combined skills of these various tradesmen provided the fort with shelter, furniture, transportation and tools, and the resources they provided benefited the Company as well. For their pains they were allotted housing attached to their working quarters which, though cramped, was a step above the bachelors' or married men's lodgings.

Blacksmiths located at all Hudson's Bay Company forts were responsible for such hardware as nails, bolts, farm implements and fireplace utensils, as well as various repair jobs to kettles, pots, knives and guns. The blacksmith at Fort Edmonton had several other duties as well as the ones already mentioned.

Edmonton being the centre of the York boat building, the blacksmith of the fort was also required to make stemplates and

Blacksmith's shop

sternplates for the boats, as well as such sundry ironwork as rudder irons, oarlocks and nails.

The Fort Edmonton blacksmith was also expected to act as farrier to the herd of packhorses bred at the fort for the Company service, as well as Rowand's own herd of racing stock animals. Horseshoes, stirrups, horse collars, brands and saddles were all constructed in the shop located directly behind his living quarters.

These specific duties aside, he was also responsible for general repairs about the fort, for building portable sheet iron stoves to heat the buildings through the long winters. His services were also available to the local Indians who needed traps, guns and tools repaired occasionally. One would assume this workload to be more than enough, but apparently sometimes the urge to moonlight was stronger than the need for sleep. An account from the 1834 Fort Edmonton Post Journal attests to this:

> Gave Annal (the boatbuilder) and the blacksmith a reprimand for working during the night with the Company's iron, wood & tools and selling what they made to the men. The latter is the worst but neither is able to sit up all night and do his duty for the Company in the day.

The York boat builders were usually natives of the Orkney Islands of Scotland — strong, hardy men descended from the Norse conquerors of the far Hebrides. Orkney fishing vessels, the prototypes of the Hudson's Bay York boats, were themselves fashioned after the ancient Norse galleys with two pointed ends.

A York boat in action

On first portage, Slave River

Because of their ability to carry large volumes of freight with minimal crew, York boats were favoured over the smaller, lighter canoes. A single York boat could carry up to 6,300 pounds, as well as eight crew members, and still draw only two feet of water. The main disadvantage of the York boats was that they were difficult to portage. Roads had to be cut ten feet wide, with roller logs set three feet apart along the road. Crew members were expected to carry two pieces, weighing approximately ninety pounds each, as they maneuvered the unwieldy boats down the portage road.

Due to the fact that they were manufactured from soft wood, the average life span of a York boat was three major trips. Emergency repair kits of planks, pitch and nails were a necessary part of the cargo. Because of the boats' relatively short life span,

Portaging a boat over a mountain portage, Slave River

Making of a York boat

boat builders at Fort Edmonton were kept constantly busy maintaining the fleet. Anywhere from five to ten York boats would be built every year in the boat shed next to the blacksmith's shop.

A fort was staffed with one of two types of woodworker — a carpenter or a joiner, who was considered a specialist in finer work such as cabinetry. The carpenter at Fort Edmonton was likely to be of the latter group, judging from the fine work in the Big House.

The carpenter was not merely a rough tradesman. He was both architect and foreman of a given project, and he shouldered his load as a common labourer. He would have been responsible

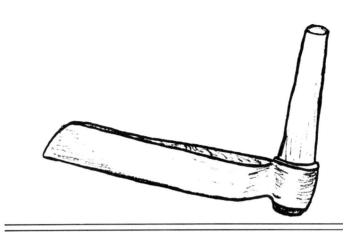

Froe used for making shingles

for furniture making, window and door work, the making of wooden implements like oars and plows, the construction of dog and horse sleds and the designing and construction of any tools he might require that were not provided by the Company. A fur post carpenter, like the blacksmith, had to combine the various attributes of skill, craft, inventiveness, versatility and (it would seem) magic. At any rate it was their work that enhanced the Indians' awe of white man's magic in their pristine domain.

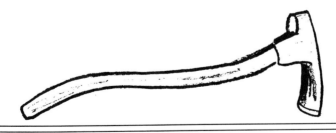

Carpenter's adze

Of course, as well as being responsible for the construction of the forts and their various contents, a Hudson's Bay carpenter had an ever-continuing job of maintaining and repairing the northwest forts. The role of the carpenter, like that of the York boat builder, was often filled by an Orkneyman. Men from the Orkneys had been signing on with the Hudson's Bay Company since as early as 1714. They were diligent and strong, and were not unaccustomed to a harsh environment. It was very likely that Stromness, a small town in the Orkney Islands from which the Company ships departed, was the largest town these young men had ever seen. With no taste of big city life behind them, they were not likely to feel isolated when placed in the far Saskatchewan District.

Although Company pay was not lucrative, it was enough to continue to draw men from the Orkneys. Since there was nothing to spend their pay on during their service to the Company, men were able, after a few years of service, to return with enough savings to set themselves up as independent crofters or fishermen. Many ex-Company men returned to the Isle of Harray in the Orkneys and were known by the other inhabitants as the "peerie [little] lairds o' Harray" because of their independent status.

Not all Orkneymen returned to the islands after their years with the Company. Many developed a great love for their new home and settled with their mixed-blood wives in the Red River Settlement. Good Orkney names like Sinclair, Isbister, Kennedy, Clouston, Ballenden and Rae are still common in the western provinces of Canada.

The cooper, or barrelmaker, was another craftsman employed by the Hudson's Bay Company for his indispensable skills. Kegs and barrels were used by the Company for shipping such delicacies as salted buffalo tongue and beaver tail, as well as for storage within the fort. The cooper was also responsible for making tubs and buckets for fort use.

Another use for the small kegs the cooper was kept busy mak-

Red River cart

Cooper's froe

Cooper's adze

ing was not quite so laudable as the shipping of salted buffalo tongues. Trade liquor, an item Indians would trade anything to get, was shipped out to the posts in large casks, and there it was placed in the cooper's fort-built kegs, often cut by as much as a third with water. When competition was high between the Hudson's Bay Company and the North West Company, trading liquor was often the deciding factor to lure recalcitrant Indians.

Being the Honourable Company, the Hudson's Bay Company tried to phase out rum as a trading item after the amalgamation in 1821, but it was so much in demand that rather than risk losing their Indians to the American traders to the south, the Company could only ration the portions rather than obliterate the substance from their trading posts.

Labourers who weren't skilled in a particular craft acted as helpers to the tradesmen and performed the menial tasks around the posts such as maintaining the forts' supplies of lumber, firewood, ice and water. These labourers usually doubled as voyageurs for the spring runs to York Factory; but some, for example the cooks, gardeners and Big House servants, remained at the forts year-'round, along with the tradesmen.

Sawing planks

SEVEN
COUNTRY WIVES

I HAD SEEN VERY FEW PLACES IN THE COUNTRY WHERE DOMESTIC ARRANGEMENTS, EITHER WITHIN DOORS OR WITHOUT, WERE CONDUCTED WITH SO MUCH PROPRIETY AS AT THIS PLACE. AT ALMOST EVERY OTHER POST, MEN AND WOMEN ARE TO BE SEEN CONGREGATING TOGETHER DURING THE SPORTS AND AMUSEMENTS OF THE MEN, AND THE WOMEN ARE OFTEN SEEN FLIRTING IDLY ABOUT THEIR ESTABLISHMENTS, MIXING TOGETHER AMONG THE MEN AT THEIR SEVERAL DUTIES. BUT IT IS NOT SO HERE; I DID NOT NOTICE A WOMAN, OLD OR YOUNG, GOING ABOUT THE PLACE IDLE; ALL SEEMED TO KEEP AT HOME AND TO BE EMPLOYED ABOUT THEIR OWN AFFAIRS. THE MORAL AND PLEASING EFFECT WAS SUCH AS MIGHT BE EXPECTED, AND REFLECTS GREAT CREDIT ON MR. ROWAND AND ON HIS FAMILY.

Alexander Ross,
found in Many Tender
Ties,
by Sylvia van Kirk, p. 132

COUNTRY WIVES

Although the days were long and arduous in the employ of the Company, many men found the nights longer. Taking a wife *a la façon du pays* became the custom. Although some men had their vows to their Indian or mixed-blood partners consecrated by the incoming missionaries, it was common practice to retire to civilization and a white wife after making a modicum of provision for the discarded "copper beauty".

In order to assure provisions for a country wife within the fort, both man and woman were required to appear before the Chief Factor to announce their intention. While Indian girls may have considered life much easier within the fort, by today's standards there was little luxury to be found in endless days of duty and drudgery. Women of the fort were not only required to care for their husbands and families, but were expected to work at the upkeep of the fort as well.

Since Edmonton was the central supplier of pemmican for

both the brigades on their way to trap and the voyageurs on their summer trip to York Factory, the women of the fort were kept busy manufacturing enormous amounts of this staple food. Pemmican could be eaten cold or as a stew called "rubaboo". A mere handful could keep a trapper going for an entire day.

To make this essential food, the women would cut buffalo meat into very thin strips and hang them on hooks or a rack over a slow, smoky fire. The fire was used mainly to keep flies off the fresh meat. After a day or two the fire was discontinued and the meat was allowed to dry in the sun and wind. Three or four times a day the women would crack the meat open to allow the outsides of the strips to dry. After the drying process, which took about a week, the meat was broken into small pieces and put inside a flour sack. The women then pounded the meat into powder. This powder was mixed with dried berries, and melted buffalo fat was used to bind the substance together into balls. The pemmican balls were then placed into bags made of green (untanned) buffalo hide, and sewn up tightly. A bag of pemmican, made properly, could be cached in the ground for several years and still remain usable.

Rubaboo is the name for a stew made of pemmican and any wild vegetables at hand. Boiled in a pot of water, the chunks of pemmican would fall apart. Additions – the likes of onion, turnip, asparagus, parsley, sage, bullrush root, cattail heads, dandelion root, wild parsnip, wild carrot, mushrooms, pine nuts, daylily roots, or wild rice – would turn it into an appetizing stew.

Fish caught at Lac Ste. Anne by the fort's crew of fishermen would be dried on the same style of rack as the buffalo strips. The women would split the fish from the tail and hang them over the rack like clothespins.

While fresh meat was preferred, and as many as a hundred carcasses could be stored on ice in the meat house, it was advisable to dry and preserve as much as possible, for the often violent winters could make animals scarce.

Supplies were sent to the forts from England via York Factory, but many items that even the poorest Dickensian waif took for granted were produced by the women of the fort. A case in point is soap. Lye soap used to scrub floors, clothing and faces was made by a process that took three or four days. A layer of straw was placed in the bottom of a leaching barrel to act as a filter. One or two bushels of ashes (hardwood ashes were found to be the best) were then placed in the barrel. Three or four gallons of hot water were poured over the ashes and left to stand overnight. The resulting liquid which drained through the straw to the bucket below was lye, a potent cleaner. In order to make soap, three pounds of fat for every quart of lye was melted and set aside to cool. When cooled nearly to its setting point, the lye was added to the fat. To insure a smooth mixture and in order to prevent splashing the lethal liquid, the lye was always added to the fat, never the fat to the lye. The mixture was then stirred over a low fire until it was the consistency of thick honey, and then poured into wooden trays lined with cheesecloth. It would take the substance two or three days to harden, after which it was turned out and cut into bars. In small doses lye soap is safe on the skin, but very abrasive if used excessively. The hands of the women who scrubbed the wooden floors of the fort were probably permanently red and raw. The floors themselves would probably shine white, though unvarnished, because of the bleaching properties of the lye.

While a husband was responsible for keeping a roof over his family's heads, it was the wife who put clothes on their backs. Soft leather moccasins were the best footwear for the wilds, but a hunter could go through a pair of these a day on an arduous trip. His wife was kept busy chewing leather to soften it for shaping into the comfortable slipper-like shoes. Leather clothing in styles adapted from those of the local Indians was long-wearing and useful as camouflage while hunting and trapping; but sturdy Hudson's Bay blankets were also used for hooded coats and leggings.

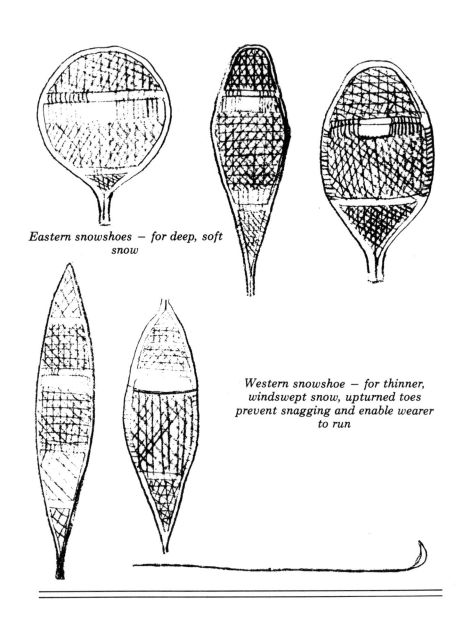

Eastern snowshoes — for deep, soft snow

Western snowshoe — for thinner, windswept snow, upturned toes prevent snagging and enable wearer to run

Women were also responsible for making the ever-essential snowshoes. Snowshoes are large, racquet-shaped devices which, when strapped onto a man's feet, enable him by means of weight displacement to walk over snowdrifts without sinking. Women fashioned a supple bough of wood into the shape of a teardrop and tied it securely with animal sinew. Next, they wove sinew across the frame into a web-like pattern, leaving a gap for the ball of the foot. The snowshoes were strapped onto moccasined feet by means of a leather thong through the webbing. Once he became adapted to the duck-like gait that snowshoes necessitated, a man could travel quickly across winter landscapes, even using his snowshoes as skis down minor slopes.

A man's worth as a trapper was often reckoned by the finery of his wardrobe. The wife of a skilled and valuable trapper or hunter was often allowed the leisure to apply herself to intricate beadwork for his apparel. Indian women had long used porcupine quills to enliven their handiwork, but the arrival of the fur trade brought brightly-coloured beads and ribbons which were quickly assimilated into intricate and beautiful patterns on moccasins, jackets, rifle-holsters and the like.

During the summer months when the winter's accumulation of furs was being conveyed down the Saskatchewan to York Factory, the northwest forts were left to the care of a skeleton staff of three or four men and the women. While life may have been dull with the men gone, it certainly wasn't restful. Women of the northwest forts were the first farmers of what is now Canada's prime agricultural area. At Fort Edmonton, a yearly average of sixteen hundred bushels of potatoes was planted, hoed and harvested, as well as barley, turnips and hay for the horses. Two fields of wheat were also sown around May 3rd and harvested sometime between September 25th and October 1st. One hundred and thirty-five days was hardly enough time for wheat to mature, so when hardier strains were finally developed they were welcomed with enthusiasm.

Major cleaning of the forts took place during the spring when they were relatively empty, and while the women weren't sewing for their men they made shirts and garments out of whole cloth from the Company for trading purposes.

There was no question that women could work just as hard as the men and were, indeed, expected to. That is where any thought of equality ended. Men ate separately and before women, and they received larger shares of fresh meat. Women were relegated to separate and smaller dining rooms even in the Factor's house. The custom of following behind included even major celebrations. On New Year's Day the men were invited to the Hall to receive "shrub, Rum and cakes" from the Factor and his family. After the men had paid their respects they left, and only then did the ladies enter. They were each kissed by the Chief Factor, *a la mode du pays*, and offered a small drink. Once the ladies had received their libations, the gentlemen feasted. Then the ladies were allowed to eat, and finally they all joined in a non-segregated dance. It must be remembered that many of these customs had been borrowed from the Indian lifestyles that these women were accustomed to. Even the *putting off* or leaving of a country wife was a common Indian practice. If a man decided to follow his tribe to hunt and his wife did not wish to follow, she had the right to return to her family as a *grass widow*. Practices that might seem inhuman and uncaring by today's standards were practical and went unquestioned by the Canadians of the eighteenth and nineteenth centuries.

It seems, however, that women joined to men of the servant class were much more secure than those in the company of Gentlemen. Many of the Orkneymen who worked as carpenters, smiths and boatmen took their Indian families back to the Hebrides with them. Others preferred to settle with their families in the Red River colony after their term of duty. Perhaps it is true that they were not responsible for the upkeep of an upperclass name, and so could afford to remain with their country spouses who had tended for them through the lean and dangerous times; but from a modern perspective many smiths and indentured servants displayed more innate humanity than others like Sir George Simpson, who had at least three native "wives" before he brought his young cousin Frances out to be his bride. After leaving one woman in York Factory he wrote back these instructions:

> If you can dispose of the Lady it will be
> satisfactory as she is an unnecessary and ex-
> pensive appendage. I see no fun in keeping a
> Woman without enjoying her charms which my
> present rambling Life does not enable me to do;
> but if she is unmarketable I have no wish that
> she should be a general accommodation shop to
> all the young bucks at the Factory.

The lady in question, Betsey Sinclair, was married off to a young Hudson's Bay Company clerk named Robert Miles. Yet, to give Simpson his due, he was the man responsible for making sure there were provisions made for country wives who were left behind. A man who made his commitment known to the Chief Factor was expected to have a portion of his pension left at the trading post, so that his ex-wife could trade there even if she could no longer live within the fort proper.

Indian women who came to live at the fort traded their native costumes for what became known as "Canadian fashion" dress — that is, a shirt, a short gown, petticoat and leggings; but they maintained their custom of using a blanket as cloak, hood and covering. These blankets, holding as they did the smoky smell of countless fires, probably helped to ward off mosquitoes and blackflies, and no amount of persuasion could keep the women from this habit. As well, they stuck to their tradition of keeping their babies wrapped in a papoose, or backpack filled with soft moss. The baby would go everywhere with its mother, strapped comfortably on her back, and the soft moss acted as an ingenious forerunner to disposable diapers.

Indian women who were *put off* managed much better than their mixed-blood successors, for they were tougher and did not take the trouble to adapt as conventionally to life within the fort. Since they had squatted on the hard-packed floors of the married men's quarters, it was no physical hardship to return to squatting

Examples of dress taken from sketches by artist Rindisbacher
(Beaver, *September 1952*)

on the floor of a teepee. Their society was one acclimatized to the possibilities of widowhood or separation, and they were prepared to survive by their own wits. Mixed-blood daughters of Gentlemen of the Company were brought up knowing only the hard chores indigenous to fort life, and likely dreamt of the faraway places their fathers remembered with such fondness. To be left to their own devices without a husband to care for them, or a father remaining in the territory, would remain a fearful prospect.

EIGHT
REVEREND ROBERT T. RUNDLE

DO NOT COMMUNICATE TO PRIVATE AND IRRESPONSIBLE PARTIES WHAT IN THE FIRST INSTANCE AT LEAST SHOULD BE COMMUNICATED TO THE SECRETARY AND COMMITTEE ALONE.

YOU WILL RECEIVE AS A SINGLE MAN 30 SPANISH DOLLARS OR £ 6.15.0 PER QUARTER AND £ 1.10.0 FOR WASHING AND STATIONERY. BE LABOURERS OF GOD AND YOU WILL BE PROVIDED FOR BY HIS CHURCH.

TAKE HEED TO YOURSELVES AS WELL AS TO YOUR DOCTRINE. KEEP YOURSELVES PURE. KEEP AT THE UTMOST DISTANCE FROM ALL TRIFLING AND LEVITY IN YOUR INTERCOURSE WITH YOUNG PERSONS, MORE ESPECIALLY WITH FEMALES. TAKE NO LIBERTIES WITH THEM. CONVERSE WITH THEM VERY SPARINGLY AND ONLY FOR RELIGIOUS PURPOSES; EVEN THEN DO NOT CONVERSE WITH THEM ALONE.

NEVER BE UNEMPLOYED. NEVER BE TRIFLINGLY EMPLOYED. DO NOT WHILE AWAY TIME...THE COMPLETION OR FRUSTRATION OF YOUR NEW MISSION MAINLY DEPENDS UNDER GOD UPON YOUR FIDELITY.

MAY THE PRESENCE OF THE GOD OF ISAAC ACCOMPANY YOU.

(Wesleyan Missionary Notices, Feb 1841, 439)

REVEREND ROBERT T. RUNDLE

Robert Terrill Rundle arrived in the Saskatchewan District in 1840. John Rowand had written to George Simpson about the need for a man of the cloth, but Rundle was not quite what he had expected. Rowand was not prepared for a twenty-nine-year-old greenhorn who would insist on paying more attention to the surrounding tribes of Indians than the members of the Company and their families within the fort. To give Rundle credit, he did not remain a greenhorn for long. He adapted quickly to the new world he found himself a part of and his eight years in the northwest were both hardworking and productive.

Rundle was born in Mylor, Cornwall in 1811. Although raised in the Curch of England, his maternal grandfather William Carvosso was a famous Methodist lay preacher, and his uncle Benjamin was a Methodist missionary in New South Wales. Grandfather William came to live with the Rundles when Robert was three and remained until he died in 1835. It was Robert's elder

The Rev. R.T. Rundle

brother William who first found God at the feet of his grandfather and prepared for life as a man of the cloth. William's dream never came true, as he died two years later; but Robert did not follow his brother's lead into mission life until some twelve years later.

First he enrolled in a business training school and busied himself with politics. It eventually led him to Wesleyan Reform. He liked the attitude of charity and missionary zeal he found among the Wesleyans. Although Rundle cherished a partiality for the Anglican faith, or "the Mother Church" as he called it − and wished to be buried eventually in Mylor Churchyard − he was pleased to be known as a Methodist, and was "proud of the name of a Wesleyan".

Rundle was accepted as a candidate for the ministry in 1839 and had been at the Training College only a few months when, as his daughter Mary later reported, "there came an urgent request from some of the Hudson's Bay Co. officials for a young man to go out as a missionary to the Indians in the far west & to act as a Company chaplain in the same District. He at once offered to go and was accepted."

It seems that the main reason the Hudson's Bay Company was supporting an influx of Wesleyan missionaries was a fear that the Roman Catholic priests who had been coming to the territory, supported as they were by the French government, would turn the Indians away from the Honourable British Company. The Wesleyans had a powerful influence in England, and could reasonably be expected to keep the Indians from migrating from workable trapping land to the missions located at the Red River Settlement. Wesleyans were welcomed into the territory with open arms, but learned quickly that they were expected to play by Company rules.

To say that Rundle's presence in Fort Edmonton was resented would seem too harsh. He was quite simply an anomaly in a northwest fort, he served no purpose to trade or survival, and the souls he logged in his book as baptized and married could not be valued in terms of "made beaver". At the same time he was being housed and fed and treated with the respect due a Gentleman of the Company. His refusal to travel on a Sunday was tolerated, but most men saw it as a sign of comparative frailty rather than an indication of spirituality. As his business was with their souls alone, his interference in the treatment and condition of natives was not welcomed. John Rowand seems to have liked Rundle as well as any missionary he came across, but the business of running the District was always to come first in Rowand's mind. He stated his opinions of Rundle in a letter to Sir George Simpson, dated January 4, 1841:

You must not be anxious about Rev. Mr. Rundale. He is well here and doing all the good he can. In my opinion the man is too young for them. It takes nothing of his worth for I believe him to be a good man. ...these tribes expect to see something superior.

The raw Scotchmen who are here are the only people who will not attend when Mr. Rundale is preaching...they keep off from him as far as they can. They are an awkward bit and as lazy as can be. The minister is in my way. I cannot go on with such a fellow as when I am alone.

...with regard to Mr. Rundale, when I say he is too young, you must understand what I mean. All the natives expect to see something in these men truly respectable and grand, superior to the Indian trader.

I have nothing but good to say of this man.

(H.B.C. Archives, D5/6)

Rowand, a Catholic, did seem to respect Rundle. He had a chapel built for him within the fort palisades, and his three unmarried daughters were partially educated by Rundle.

The young missionary also developed a great friendship with James Harriott, Rowand's son-in-law and Chief Trader in Rocky Mountain House. Harriott, with his knowledge of Indian dialects, helped to translate many of Rundle's sermons. He also helped to introduce Rundle to the various tribes located around Rocky Mountain House.

One of Rundle's interpreters who wasn't a great help to him was Jamie Jock Bird, the half-breed son of the late Chief Factor James Bird of Red River. Since his father's death Jamie Jock's status had lowered considerably in the territory, and he was renowned as a troublemaker. His intelligence and facility with In-

Jamie Jock Bird

dian dialects would have made him an ideal choice as an inter-
preter but, apparently, he chose not only to interpret but to em-
broider and proselytize on his own. When Rundle accused him of
this, Jamie Jock humiliated him in the midst of a great gathering
of Blackfoot by refusing to interpret at all. Rundle never quite got
over this humiliation and, although his relationship with the Cree
flourished, he always seemed a bit off-balance when dealing with
members of the Blackfoot Confederacy. Oddly enough, Jamie
Jock and Rundle continued a relationship through the years based
on friendship as much as mutual need.

Governor Simpson was often at odds with the Wesleyans in
the Company territory. On the one hand he hated the in-

terferences of Superintendent Evans at Norway House. On the other he was equally irritated by Rundle's habitual disappearances from Fort Edmonton to visit Indians in their camps. He wrote of his feelings to Evans after having missed seeing Rundle at Edmonton House while en route to the Pacific in 1841:

> I am much disappointed at not having fallen in with Mr. Rundle who I think would do much more good by remaining at one or the other of the Establishments or dividing his time amongst them, than in wandering about the country in search of Indians at their camps. There I am certain he can do no good, especially among the Plains Indians while he exposes himself & us to insult and ridicule...employing Jamie Jock, one of the most worthless of his breed in the country as his interpreter...Mr. Rundle from what I have heard of him, possesses more zeal than judgement; he is nevertheless well spoken of & much liked by Mr. Rowand & the different other Gentlemen of the District...Mr. Rundle I regret to learn is not quite so grave and serious in his manner as would be desirable...and is too much given to frivolous chit chat and gossip with our Clerks and others, & is rather indiscreet in the expression of his opinions on the mode of management or dealing with the natives, matters on which he must from his experience be perfectly incompetent to form an opinion.
>
> (WMS Archives Box 12/1)

Despite the criticisms Rundle continued to visit the tribes on their own ground, and eventually founded a mission in the Battle River area near Pigeon Lake.

Superintendent Evans, located at Norway House, had a colourful career in the Hudson's Bay territory. His development of a Cree written syllabic system should have been heralded as a major missionary triumph, but that and his other good works were shadowed by the ignominious way in which he was removed from his mission. At the same time that Sir George Simpson was complaining about his interference, Evans was accused of various sexual offences by members of the Norway House and Rossville communities. He was found not guilty of the charges, but reprimanded for being imprudent. He was removed to England and subjected to another Wesleyan Society trial. Evans was eventually acquitted but died of a massive heart attack before the verdict was announced.

Whether Evans was guilty, imprudent, or merely misunderstood, he will be remembered as the man who invented a much-appreciated communications tool for the Plains Cree. During a visit to Edmonton in 1841 he taught the system to Rundle who, with James Harriott's help, was able to translate the Lord's Prayer and other common scriptures into the Indians' own language. The syllabic system resembles hieroglyphics. It is a clear and simple method for transcribing the language of the Plains Cree, one of the largest groups of Indians to traffic in the area of Fort Edmonton.

Key to the Cree Syllabic System

	as in hate ā		as in pin e		as in no o		as in pun u		as in pan a		Final Consonants
VOWELS		ᐁ		ᐃ		ᐅ		ᐊ		ᐋ	
W	wā	ᐍ	we	ᐏ	wo	ᐓ	wu	ᐘ	wa	ᐚ	
P	pā	ᐯ	pe	ᐱ	po	ᐳ	pu	ᐸ	pa	ᐹ	ᑊ
T	tā	ᑌ	te	ᑎ	to	ᑐ	tu	ᑕ	ta	ᑖ	ᐟ
K	kā	ᑫ	ke	ᑭ	ko	ᑯ	ku	ᑲ	ka	ᑳ	ᐠ
CH	chā	ᒉ	che	ᒋ	cho	ᒍ	chu	ᒐ	cha	ᒑ	ᐨ
M	mā	ᒣ	me	ᒥ	mo	ᒧ	mu	ᒪ	ma	ᒫ	ᒼ
N	nā	ᓀ	ne	ᓂ	no	ᓄ	nu	ᓇ	na	ᓈ	ᐣ
S	sā	ᓭ	se	ᓯ	so	ᓱ	su	ᓴ	sa	ᓵ	ᐢ
Y	yā	ᔦ	ye	ᔨ	yo	ᔪ	yu	ᔭ	ya	ᔮ	

<u>Extra signs</u>

X = Christ
ᕒ = r
ᓬ = l
: = wi
" = h before a vowel
" = soft guttural h when before a consonant

Final oo ... °
Final i ... •
Aspirated final k ... ˣ

ᓂᐳᒎᐁ.   23. ᕽ ᑎᐅᐱᒋᖅ ᐁᑲ ᐃᒪᐅᒡᐳᑎᖅᵗ; ᐁᒪᐃᕀ ᖃᕽᵢ ᓂ ᕽ ᑊᐧᒪᓚᑉ.
         ᓂ ᐱᒡᔪᐁᗋ ᐊᐧ ᐁᕽᐧᖁᐧᓯᐧᕽᕀ; ᓂᕽ ᐃᐦᐧᒪᕽ ᕐᗠ
         ᐁ ᑊᔭᒋ ᐧᔭᑊ ᓂᐱᕀ.
         ᕌᐧᒋᐧᐊᗬ ᓂᕽ ᐧᒡᕽᕽ; ᓂ ᑊᑊᗌᐧᐃᐧ ᕽᔭᕽᕽᑎᕌ ᕐᕽᐌᕽ ᐅ
         ᐃᐧᑊᐃᕀ ᐅᕽᕐ.
         ᐁᐧᐧ, ᕽᕀ ᐃᑌᐅᕀᗋ ᕽᕀᑎᐊᕽ ᐊᕽ ᐧ ᕽᕽᕽᐅᕽᖃᕽ ᓂᕀᐃᕀᐧ
         ᐁᒪ ᖃᕽᵢ ᕽ ᐃᕀᕽᕽ ᓂ ᕽ ᕽᕽᐅᕀᕽ; ᕐᖃᗌ ᑊ ᐃᕀᖃᕀᕽᕽ; ᑊ ᕀᗋᖁᕽ
         ᐃᐧᐧᕽᕽᕽ ᕌᐁ ᑊ ᕽᕽᕽᗬᐧᐧᕽᕽᕽ ᓂ ᓂᕽᕽᕐᕽᕽᗫᕽᕀ.
         ᕽᔭᕽᕽᐃᕌᗬᕀ ᕌᕀᗬᐧᕽᗬᕽᕽ ᐧ ᕽᑲᐧᕽᐳᕌᕐᕽ ᕽ ᐃᕀ ᓂᗬᕽᗬᕽᑊᗋᕽᕽᕽ;
         ᑊ ᑊ ᕽᕀᕽᗋᗋᐧᕽ ᓂᕽᑎᕽᕽᕀ ᐱᕐ ᗩᕽᕐᕽ; ᓂ ᕌᐅᕽᕽᕀ ᕽᕀᕽᐧᐁᕽᗬᕀᕽ.
         ᕌᕀᗫᕽᑎᕌᗬᕀ ᕌᐁ ᑊᕀᕽᗋᗋᕽᕀᕀ ᒪ ᐃᕀ ᓂ ᕽ ᐃᕌᑎᕽᕽᐧᕽᕀ
         ᐃᕀᗋᕽᕫ ᕽ ᐃᒪᑎᕀᕀᕃ; ᐧᕽᕈ ᕽ ᑎᐅᐱᒋᖅᕀ ᐅ ᕽᕽᕽᐧᐃᕽᑲᓂᕽᕀ ᓂ ᕽ
         ᐃᐧᑊᕀ ᕽᑊᕴ.

23. 1 The Lord is my shepherd;
      I shall not want.
   2 He maketh me to lie down in
      green pastures: he leadeth me
      beside the still waters.
   3 He restoreth my soul: he leadeth
      me in the paths of righteousness
      for his name's sake.
   4 Yea, though I walk through the
      valley of the shadow of death, I
      will fear no evil: for thou art
      with me; thy rod and thy staff
      they comfort me.
   5 Thou preparest a table before me
      in the presence of mine enemies:
      thou anointest my head with oil;
      my cup runneth over.
   6 Surely goodness and mercy shall
      follow me all the days of my life:
      and I will dwell in the house of
      the Lord for ever.

Rundle's greatest sense of achievement came from his friendship with the Indians, and with one in particular. Maskepetoon, a Cree chief, acted as Rundle's sponsor and helped to arrange meetings with migratory tribes. In 1844 he sent his son to Rundle with a letter. "My son Bejamin I would like to learn English." Benjamin Maskepetoon became a constant companion. The young man was with Rundle when the missionary, as legend has it, climbed the mountain named after him near the present town of Banff.

Rundle does not make much of his mountaineering feat in his own journals, but years later the Rev. J.T.F. Halligey wrote of the event:

> Climbing the formidable heights of 10,000 feet
> with frequent interruptions of snowstorm and
> fog...soon after passing the summit, a very
> dense fog enveloped (Rundle's party), and the
> intrepid missionary was suddenly seized with a
> fear which forbade him taking another step. So
> he picked up a stone and threw it in front. In a
> few moments he heard it drop thousands of
> feet below. He then realized he was on the edge
> of a huge precipice.

In 1848 a weary and homesick Rundle was released from duty and travelled home to England. The British Wesleyan Society handed over responsibility of the territory to the Canadian Conference, and Rundle's wish to return to British North America was never fulfilled. Neither were his plans to continue his mission work in Australia. In 1854 he married Mary Wolverson, and together they had nine children. Rundle died and was buried in Garstang, Lancashire on Feb. 4, 1896 at the age of eighty-five. His life had been one of merit and service; fifty-seven years devoted to the Wesleyan Methodist Church. For eight of those years he was a missionary in one of the most unruly and least civilized areas of Rupert's Land.

NINE
THE INDIANS

ALL OUR STORIES ARE ABOUT A BEING WHO WAS A SPIRIT IN THE FORM OF A HUMAN BEING. HE WAS THE FIRST BEING WHEN THE WORLD WAS MADE. SO HE WAS OLDER THAN ALL THE ANIMALS AND ALL THE PLANTS IN THE WORLD; EVERYTHING WAS HIS YOUNGER BROTHER. HE COULD TALK TO ANIMALS AND BIRDS, FISHES AND INSECTS, WATER AND WIND, TREES, ROCKS — EVERYTHING. WE CALL HIM WISAKEDJAK.

WHEN THE FIRST HUMAN BEINGS CAME, WISAKEDJAK TAUGHT THEM HOW TO KILL THE FIRST CREATURES AND WHAT USE TO MAKE OF THEM.

"NOW TAKE THEM AND USE THEM AS NATURE PLANNED," WISAKEDJAK TOLD THE NEW PEOPLE. "THERE IS TO BE NO CRUELTY TOWARD THEM — EVER. YOU MUST TEACH YOUR CHILDREN AND YOUR CHILDREN'S CHILDREN HOW TO CATCH THEM AND HOW TO USE THEM. THEY MUST BE TREATED KINDLY."

OUR ELDER BROTHER ALSO TAUGHT THE HUMAN PEOPLE WHAT ROOTS TO USE FOR FOOD AND WHAT HERBS TO USE FOR SICKNESS. "THESE WERE MADE TO BE GOOD AND TO BE TRULY USEFUL. DO NOT WASTE THEM. ALWAYS LEAVE SOME OF THE ROOTS FOR NEXT YEAR'S CROP. NEVER DIG ALL OF THE ROOTS."

WISAKEDJAK INTENDED THAT EVERYTHING SHOULD LAST FOREVER, AND YET HE PREDICTED THE COMING OF THE WHITE MAN. "ANOTHER RACE OF PEOPLE WILL COME," HE SAID. "THEY WILL KILL ALL THE BUFFALOES. THEY WILL DESTROY THE TWELVE FOOD PLANTS THAT GROW ALONG THE EDGE OF THE MOUNTAINS. THEY WILL WASTE THE FORESTS."

EVERYTHING HAS COME TO PASS AS OUR ELDER BROTHER PREDICTED.

From Indian Legends in Canada, *compiled by Ella Elizabeth Clark, 1960, McClelland & Stewart*

THE INDIANS

The fur trade, while providing the Indians with overwhelming technological advancements, was ultimately responsible for the end of a way of life. Indian expertise in trapping and survival was necessary to the fur trading companies. In consequence the indigenous people of Canada fared better at the hands of their colonizers than many other aboriginal people of the world. Assimilation, however, was the wish of neither the Indian nor the Company. Eventually, the more powerful social structure won out.

The predominant tribes of the Saskatchewan District were the Cree – Woodland, Swampy and Plains bands; and the members of the Blackfoot Confederacy – Blackfoot, Bloods, Piegans and Sarcee. Fort Edmonton was situated to accommodate both of these warring tribes, earning it a name as the most dangerous post in the district. The local Crees and Assiniboines were considered more trustworthy than the high-spirited Blackfoot, and were often offered credit at the trading posts against their upcoming winter catches.

Buffalo

Trustworthy or not, horses were guarded closely at the fort when any Indians were in the neighbourhood. Horse stealing was looked upon as honourable by all Indian tribes, and no amount of persuasion that it was base thievery could keep them from a time-honoured tradition. Horses were fair game whether they belonged to a warring tribe, a neighbouring tribe, or the Hudson's Bay Company.

The Plains Indians were nomadic in nature, following the buffalo for their livelihood. The large shaggy wild oxen of the western plains provided much more than just a source of meat for the Indians. Grease was used for cooking, trading and the making of pemmican; sinew became thread as well as webbing for snowshoes; bones and horns could be fashioned into tools; and the thick dressed hides made warm blankets.

Before guns became commonplace to the Plains Indians they hunted buffalo by stampeding them over cliffs or into carefully constructed killing pens. When the buffalo were plentiful the Indians prospered. As the great herds dwindled on the plains they had once commanded, the Indians were forced to trap smaller fur-bearing animals for their new livelihood. The pelts — taken for granted by the Indians — seemed excessively prized by the white traders. Indians, with a knowledge of both the land and the animals' ways, did their best to accommodate the traders' whims.

A great many furred animals could be trapped in the northwest. Their pelts became the universal currency and the new price for articles of value. The Indians were familiar with the habits and favoured areas of all the valuable creatures living in the northwest. Badgers — thickset members of the weasel family — burrowed in the prairie wastes. Their hair was at one time used in the making of brushes. Bears — black, cinnamon and grizzly — were found in most parts of Canada. Anywhere from five to nine feet long, bear hides were commonly used as rugs and covering robes.

The bobcat and Canada lynx were (and are) the most common of the wild cats trapped in Canada. The bobcat is smaller, with reddish fur, and less valuable than the silvery lynx. Lynx often weigh as much as forty pounds and sport thick, fluffy coats. Broad padded feet enable them to be very fleet in the winter.

The robes of kings are usually trimmed in ermine, the fur of one of the most ferocious small animals in Canada. Reddish-brown in the summer months, ermines turn snowy white in the winter. Only the tip of the tail remains black year-round. Ermines are elongated, short-legged nimble creatures of the weasel family and

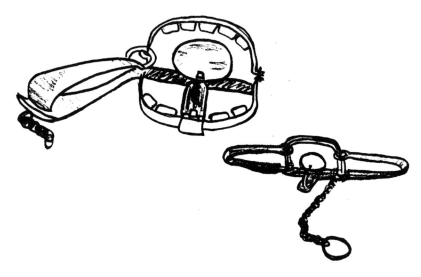

Skunk and muskrat traps

Offset jaw beaver trap

are quite fearless, attacking and killing animals much larger than themselves.

The marten and his larger cousin the fisher are unsociable animals found in the densely-forested areas of Canada. The colour of the marten's silky fur ranges from yellow to rich brown, while the fisher is sometimes almost black. Female fisher skins are more valuable than the larger male skins.

The first Indian trappers found mink, the quintessential luxury fur, to be plentiful in the Canadian Shield even without the advantage of today's mink ranches. The mink, also of the weasel family, is slightly larger than the ermine. The male is usually twice as large as the female, weighing up to four pounds. The softer, smaller female skins are considered more valuable.

The muskrat is built like an economy-model beaver. It is also an amphibious rotent, but its long, bare, vertically-flattened tail is much narrower than the beaver's. Muskrat hind feet are webbed to help it swim through its marshy environment. A combination of guard hairs and downy underhairs keep the muskrat warm in cold waters. Like the beaver's, its fur can be used for felt as well as fur coats, but it is much smaller than its sixty-pound relative.

Otters are among the most valued members of the weasel family to inhabit the Canadian forests. They are always found near a lake or large river and are the most aquatic of the weasels. Otters are generally considered the most intelligent and sociable members of the family.

Of the wild dog family the prairie wolf, fox and timber wolf are the most common to the Canadian Shield. Also known as the coyote, the prairie wolf is slender, fleet and difficult to trap. It has coarse greyish-yellow fur with a few black hairs along its back. The timber wolf is much larger and heavier. Southern timber wolves have similar markings to coyotes, but the more northerly wolves often bear fur that is almost white.

The fox, trapped mainly by the woods tribes, is found in most of the forested regions of Canada. It is small and long-haired, with a long bushy tail. The red fox is the most common and is identified by its red body, black legs and ears and white-tipped tail. The cross or patch fox is yellowish with a dark cross over the shoulders. The silver fox is black with white hairs across the back and a white-tipped tail.

The raccoon, trapped principally for coat fur, is a small member of the bear family. It lives in the south in wooded areas near lakes or marshes. Known as the "little bandit" because of its distinctive black-masked face, the raccoon has long greyish-brown fur and a black-ringed tail. Its paws have well-separated toes, and the raccoon uses its forefeet like hands.

Of the species of squirrel native to Canada only the red squirrel has any commercial importance. It is a bushy-tailed rodent which inhabits the northern coniferous forests. It has soft, brownish-red fur with a white underbelly. Squirrel pelts are commonly dyed brown before they are processed.

Wolverines, the largest and fiercest of the weasel family, are trapped not so much for their fur but because they are a plague to traplines. They commonly prey on trapped animals, destroying them before the trapper can return. Wolverine fur is customarily used as parka trim. Unlike others furs, wolverine fur does not frost up from the wearer's breath in cold weather.

The Indians did not use all the furs they trapped for trading. Furs were used to decorate their clothing and (like the wolverine trim) useful as a buffer against the severe Canadian winters. In this way they differed from the Company traders who were commanded to transport all furs traded to Europe. Trapping, while an important part of the Indians' economy, was considered an extension, not an alternative to their way of life.

While the men hunted, it often fell to the Indian women to run the traplines. They were also responsible for cleaning and tanning the pelts that were caught. This they did, along with countless other chores with their babies strapped to their backs in a pack frame known as a *papoose*. The baby was packed into the papoose, surrounded by soft moss — an early answer to disposable diapers.

Company men were often shocked at the usage the Indian men made of their women, but every member of a nomadic community must pull their load and Indian women took their lot for granted. They did all the setting-up of encampments, the cooking and the child-care. They also acted as pack-animals on long treks. If an Indian woman married into the fort, she was escaping to a somewhat easier life.

Traditionally, when an Indian woman arrived at the fort to become the wife of one of the Company men, the women of the fort would bathe her, washing the paint from her face and the grease from her hair. They would exchange her long doeskin tunic for an empire-waisted "Canada style" fabric dress. She would retain her leggings and her blanket, which was shawl, coat and headgear to her.

Indian men wore a shorter version of the same doeskin tunic, breechclouts and leggings. Their clothing was decorated with quill and beadwork, signifying their prowess as hunters. If they were successful enough to keep their wives busy with beadwork rather than having to hunt as well, their clothing boasted of their achievements.

To the chagrin of the missionaries who arrived in Indian country it was discovered that chastity was not considered a virtue, although unfaithful wives were often severely punished. According to the number of people Rundle baptized and Indian legends, the Plains Indians took readily to Christianity. There exists an Assiniboine legend about Rundle's arrival among them:

> One night a Stoney had a dream. In his dream a voice said to him, "A white man is coming to Rocky Mountain House. He will tell you about a Great Spirit you have never heard about. He works for that Great Spirit." Not long afterward, the Indian men went to Rocky Mountain

House to get knives and bullets for hunting and to get clothing for the women. When they came back, they said to the old men and to the women, "The man who works for the Great Spirit is at Rocky Mountain House. His name is Rundle." The man's dream had come true. Next day all the Stoneys went to Rocky Mountain House to see the missionary — all the men and all the women. He taught them about God. As soon as they heard this preacher, the Stoneys believed in God. They quit all their sins and followed his teachings. Ever since then, the Stoneys have been Christians. They don't want to do wrong things. They are always friendly to everyone. They love all the tribes in the world. They want to have everlasting life.
— from Mrs. Eliza Hunter, in *Indian Legends in Canada*, compiled by E.C. Clark, 1960

Oral tradition among the Indians provided much more than a continuation of history and legend. Weather prediction guides and natural remedies were also passed down from one generation to another. A few examples of weather guides are:

If the horns of the new moon are up, it will be a dry month.

If the horns of a new moon are down, it will rain for a month.

If frost comes after the maple buds, it will be a cold summer.

If pine trees have a heavy cone drop, it will be a long, hard winter.

If squirrels and dogs have heavy coats, it will be a severe winter.

While the whites in the fort made do with limited medical supplies and Factors with sparse medical knowledge, the Indians turned to natural and time-tested remedies for their ailments. Sweetgrass or "weegies" was found in marshy areas, and used as

Sweetgrass, or sweet flag (Acorus calamus)

aspirin for pain. It was chewed and held in the mouth to numb a toothache or to soothe a sore throat; could be boiled as tea for colds, and applied after chewing as a poultice to a wound as an antiseptic and a painkiller.

Green tamarack was a cure for arthritis or "sore bones". Small pieces of the tree, chopped from near the top, were boiled and the liquid was drunk. After a week of this treatment with the same sticks, the pieces of wood were then buried near their parent tree.

Other trees also provided medicinal relief. Balsam gum was extracted from the bubbles on the bark and boiled to make a tisane for coughing and sore chests. The inner bark of poplar trees was used as a poultice to take the swelling out of bee stings.

Ancient medical lore was of no use in 1837, however, when the great epidemic of smallpox swept the northwest. While the Hudson's Bay Company provided many forts with cowpox vaccine in the interests of business and humanity, it seems that Fort Edmonton did not receive any vaccine. John Rowand wrote to Sir George Simpson on December 28, 1837, that:

> ...our principal Chiefs...informed me that more than half of all the slave tribes are no more. When I mention the slave tribes you must understand it includes five different tribes all the Blackfeet, Blood Indians, Piegan, Circees and Fall Indians or Gros Ventres...their statement is very alarming indeed it cannot be more. To hear it at a long distance it may not perhaps be so striking but to us in this Country we poor Indian traders exposed and situated as we are without any Medical Assistance or anything else for the good of our Souls or Body it is most distressing and to have to witness so much misery without being able to do any good it is the more painful.
> — from "Smallpox: the Epidemic of 1837-38" by Arthur J. Ray, *The Beaver*, Autumn, 1975

The years of the epidemic must have seemed a terrifying and apocalyptic time for the Indians of the northwest. The virulent smallpox was destroying hundreds — thousands — and the white men in the fort seemed hardly affected. By 1838 only a third of the people from the great tribes that had roamed the plains were still alive.

The advent of silk top-hats was not only the end of the fur trade, but the end of a way of life for the Indians. The importance of trapping diminished, and without the demand for their special expertise the Indians discovered they were a people no longer valued.

TEN
SIR GEORGE SIMPSON

THE GOVERNOR — THE LATE SIR GEORGE SIMPSON — WAS, THOUGH NOT TALL, SAY ABOUT FIVE FEET SEVEN AT MOST, OF RATHER IMPOSING MIEN, STOUT, WELL KNIT FRAME, AND OF GREAT EXPANSE AND FULNESS OF CHEST, AND WITH AN EYE BRIGHTLY BLUE, AND EVER A BLAZE IN PEACE OR WAR, AND WITH AN ADDRESS WHICH EVER COMBINED THE "SUAVITER IN MODO, ET FORTITER IN IMPERIO". HIS WAS, INDEED, ON SUCH AN OCCASION, AN ADDRESS TO STRICK AWE ON HIS HEARERS. DURING THE FORTY YEARS THAT HE RULED THE GREAT BRITISH NORTH AMERICAN WILD, WITH ALL ITS UNTAMED SAVAGISM, AND CONDUCTED — FOR HE EVER REGULATED EVERY DETAIL OF THE TRADE — THE AFFAIRS OF THE HUDSON'S BAY COMPANY, HE PROVED HIMSELF THE "PROPER MAN IN THE PROPER PLACE," AND FEW INDEED, IF ANY, THERE COULD HAVE BEEN FOUND TO FILL IT SO WELL.

Malcolm McLeod, editor of
A Canoe Voyage from
Hudson's Bay to the
Pacific, by the late Sir
George Simpson in 1828;
(J. Durie & Son, 1872)
p. 27-28.

SIR GEORGE SIMPSON

Sir George Simpson rose from inauspicious beginnings to become one of the most important men of the nineteenth century. His strength of will forged the confused post-amalgamation fur trade into the well-oiled fur-producing machine that was the Hudson's Bay Company. The achievement lasted for one glowing generation.

Simpson was born illegitimate in Loch Broom, Scotland, where he was raised and educated by his grandfather, a clergyman. At about the age of fourteen he was sent to London to apprentice in the West Indies sugar trade. While there, he came under the eye of Andrew Wedderburn Colville, Lord Selkirk's brother-in-law. When Colville became influential in the Hudson's Bay Company, he did not forget the young clerk. George Simpson joined the Honourable Company in 1820.

Simpson was sent to the Athabaska District to work under the leadership of Colin Robertson, but on his arrival at Fort Wed-

Sir George Simpson

derburn as the H.B.C. correspondent to Fort Chipewyan, he discovered that Robertson had been kidnapped by Nor'westers and taken out of the country. It was up to Simpson, the greenhorn, to assume command of the Athabaska District.

He caught on quickly, and was attempting expansion into the New Caledonia District across the Rockies when the coalition between the companies occurred. Plans for expansion were shelved and Simpson became the Governor of the Northern District for the newly-formed Hudson's Bay Company. The Northern District extended from the U.S. border to the Arctic and reached from the Rockies on the west to the Hudson's Bay on the east. Simpson soon proved himself the best man for the job. Uncluttered by old enmities, he appeared objective among the quick-tempered "associates" who only a year before had been enemies.

With a ruthless eye for business Simpson quickly set about cutting the Company's staff by more than half and closing superfluous trading posts. He lowered wages and reduced the amount of luxury goods travelling inland for the traders' personal use. His single-handed determination turned the company into a highly profitable working venture. The governing board was suitably impressed and, in 1826, Simpson was made Governor of all the Hudson's Bay Company territories.

With fur trading once more a monopoly, the Indians could no longer enjoy the abundance of liquor and the high prices they had been demanding for their furs. Trading prices were regularized and the Indians began to look kindly upon the new amalgamation. On the other hand liquor rations were cut drastically, only continuing in those posts which competed with the whiskey-trading Americans.

While on his 1824 journey to the Pacific, Simpson decided it would be beneficial to introduce missionaries into the territory to convert the Indians. Simpson hoped the missionaries would inspire their converts to:

> ...imbibe our manners and customs and imitate us in Dress; our Supplies would thus become necessary to them which would increase the consumption of European produce & manufactures and in like measure increase & benefit our trade as they would find it requisite to become more industrious and to turn their attention more seriously to the Chase in order to be enabled to provide themselves with such supplies.
> — *Fur Trade and Empire*, Sir George Simpson
> Harvard University Press, 1931, p. 108

While he may have valued their trading potential, Simpson had no tolerance for native or mixed-blood people. Even by the standards of his day he was an uncommonly bitter racist. His bias against mixed-blood company employees was strikingly evident in his conflict with Dr. John McLoughlin, Chief of the Columbia District.

McLoughlin's mixed-blood son was Chief Trader of Fort Stikine. When McLoughlin Jr. was murdered by his men, Simpson chose to believe reports that the young man had been tyrannical and often drunk, and had been killed in self-defence by one of his servants. Even when incontestable proof was submitted to the contrary, Simpson refused to change his opinion. The Governor considered mixed-blood peoples to be lazy and unreliable, unworthy of any but the lowest positions in the Company.

Simpson also did not approve of marriages between the white traders and native or mixed-blood women. Despite this disapproval he himself had at least three relationships with such "bits of brown" and "copper beauties" during his term of office. He also disapproved of company resources being used to accommodate these liaisons within the forts, and refused to allow his new wife, Frances, to associate with such ladies, even those whose marriages had been sanctified by the missionaries. The cavalier manner with which he cast off his country wife Margaret Taylor, mother of two of his children, and brought his young cousin Frances out from England to reign as first lady of the territory, cost him the respect of many traders. Simpson did not seem to care. The "little emperor" of Rupert's Land didn't mind if his men did not like him, as long as they obeyed him. Men who displeased him were summarily transferred to obscure and terrible posts with little hope of promotion or reprieve. Rupert's Land was run for the good of the Company, and in Rupert's Land Simpson was the Company.

Simpson's exploits as a traveller have become legendary. He travelled many times across the continent of North America, several times back across the Atlantic to England and Europe, and once around the world. Where he went did not seem as important as how far he went and how quickly he managed to get there. His personal voyageurs were hand-picked both for their strength

Lady Frances Simpson

in paddling and for their ability to sing. The travelling party would often log as many as 50 miles a day. These days would begin at three in the morning, with Simpson allowing a break for breakfast after six or seven hours of paddling, and a lunch break of only an hour some time later. Simpson took pride in his travelling stamina, although he spent the time dictating to his secretary in the middle of the large canoe. He never got his feet wet either, since he was carried onto shore on the back of one of his voyageurs. It was undoubtedly an imposing sight to see the Governor arrive. He sat in state in the majestic "master's canoe", with the voyageurs singing lustily and Colin Fraser, Simpson's personal piper, playing "Scotland the Brave" or some such tune on the bagpipes.

Simpson's reputation as a prodigious traveller was of great advantage in monitoring his territory. Although he could not manage to visit every district in one season, the Factors and Traders in the outlying areas never knew when he might descend on them, and so cautiously behaved themselves against a possible visitation.

View of the Old Fort, legislative buildings and High Level bridge
1912

In his forty years with the Company, Simpson made a major voyage every year but three. He had long since proven himself to his men. One must assume that he enjoyed pitting himself against the harsh environment, and revelled in the excitement and adventure of the voyages.

In 1841 Queen Victoria conferred the title of Knight of the Bath on George Simpson. Throughout his life — a true rags-toriches story from ignominious illegitimacy to Sir George Simpson — he demonstrated the winning qualities of the quintessential self-made man.

Although he had been a strong and hardy individual all his life, Simpson's physical strength and stamina began to deteriorate in the late 1850s. In 1860, nearing death, he rallied to oversee and participate in the grand spectacle of the visit of the Prince of Wales. He kept himself alive until the visit was completed. Then, with that last feather in his cap, he surrendered to nature.

Simpson's life and death can be viewed as analogous to the great era of the fur trade in Canada. The Hudson's Bay Company reigned supreme and the fur trade rose to its peak of activity during his governorship. The year of Simpson's death, talks were already underway for the transfer of the Hudson's Bay Company holdings to the Dominion of Canada. In 1870, a decade later, the area once known as Rupert's Land became the Northwest Territories, and a new era in Canadian history began.

Bibliography

BATTLE FOR THE WEST, Daniel Francis. Hurtig Publishers (Edmonton: 1982)

BEAVER, THE (periodical), Hudson's Bay Co. (Winnipeg: 1922 -   ) quarterly.

BIBLE IN PLAIN CREE, THE, British and Foreign Bible Society (London: 1946)

FORT ASSINIBOINE, ALBERTA, 1823-1914: FUR TRADE POST TO SETTLED DISTRICT, R.F. McCarty, unpublished M.A. thesis, University of Alberta, 1976.

FUR TRADE AND EMPIRE, George Simpson, ed. F. Merk. Cambridge University Press: 1931.

FUR TRADE AT LESSER SLAVE LAKE 1815-1831, THE, W.P. Baergen, unpublished M.A. thesis, University of Alberta, 1967.

FUR TRADE OF FORT CHIPEWYAN AT LAKE ATHABASKA, 1778-1835, THE, J.M. Parker, unpublished M.A. thesis, University of Alberta, 1967.

HISTORY OF ALBERTA, A, J.G. MacGregor, Hurtig Publishers (Edmonton: rev. ed., 1981)

HISTORY OF THE CANADIAN WEST TO 1870-71, A, Arthur S. Morton, Thomas Nelson & Sons (Toronto: 1939)

HONOURABLE COMPANY, THE, Douglas McKay, McClelland & Stewart (Toronto: 1936)

INDIAN LEGENDS OF CANADA, Ella Elizabeth Clark, McClelland & Stewart (Toronto: 1960)

LITTLE EMPEROR: GOVERNOR SIMPSON OF THE HUDSON'S BAY COMPANY, THE, J.S. Galbraith, Macmillan (Toronto: 1976)

MANY TENDER TIES, Sylvia Van Kirk, Watson & Dwyer Publishing Ltd. (Winnipeg: 1980)

PEACE RIVER: A CANOE VOYAGE FROM HUDSON'S BAY TO THE PACIFIC BY THE LATE SIR GEORGE SIMPSON IN 1828, Archibald McDonald, M. McLeod, eds., J. Durie & Son (Ottawa: 1972)

JOHN ROWAND, J.G. MacGregor, Western Producer Prairie Books (Saskatoon: 1978)

RUNDLE JOURNALS 1840-1848, THE, Hugh A. Dempsey, ed., Historical Society of Alberta: 1977.

STORY OF THE TRAPPER, THE, A.C. Laut, D. Appleton & Company (New York: 1902)

STRANGERS IN BLOOD, Jennifer S.H. Brown, University of British Columbia Press: 1980.

STUDY OF THE HISTORY OF THE ROCKY MOUNTAIN HOUSE AREA, A, E.S. Gish, unpublished M.A. thesis, University of Alberta, 1952.

Index